"The Catcher in the Rye and Ph_____
*with the perfect mix of humor and intellectual insight, the
complexities and contrarieties of Salinger's timeless masterpiece,
and the whirlwind of philosophical ideas and unparalleled
charm that's made Holden Caulfield an icon for generations of
readers."*

—RICHARD ROSENBAUM, Editor, *Broken Pencil* magazine

---

*"It's the book that refuses to go away. In the seven decades since
it was first published,* The Catcher in the Rye *has become a
fixture of American pop culture and a subject of fascination to
literary critics. The thoughtful chapters suggest why thoughtful
people keep coming back to Salinger's work."*

—PAUL CANTOR, author of *Gilligan Unbound* and *The Invisible
Hand in Popular Culture*

---

*"A smart, straight-talking romp through Salinger's literary play-
ground. This is the real deal for those of us who still have a little
Holden in our hearts. Mr. Vinson wouldn't like it."*

—RAY BOSSERT, Visiting Assistant Professor at Franklin and
Marshall College

---

*"I always suspected philosophers were a bunch of phonies, but the
chapters in* The Catcher in the Rye and Philosophy *are not
crumby at all. Lively and thoughtful, these essays allow us to
examine the old high-school standard in a new light. This is the
perfect book to read on the train at night while eating a ham
sandwich."*

—ROBERT T. TALLY JR., author of *Kurt Vonnegut and the
American Novel*

"The Catcher in the Rye *is much like adolescence itself: funny, strange, heartbreaking, and absolutely essential for the journey to maturity.* The Catcher in the Rye and Philosophy *is equally smart, fun, and essential. Only phonies won't love it.*"

—RACHEL LURIA, co-editor of *Neil Gaiman and Philosophy: Gods Gone Wild!*

"*A fascinating and entertaining journey. Anyone who ever wondered where the ducks go in winter needs to read this book.*"

—KENNETH SLAWENSKI, deadcaulfields.com

"*Feeling crumby? Being a phony? That's grand. But if you're looking for all the David Copperfield kind of crap about Holden and* The Catcher in the Rye *in all of its Phoebe-like genuineness, then this is the book for you!*"

—DEAN A. KOWALSKI, author of *Moral Theory at the Movies*

The Catcher in the Rye and Philosophy

Popular Culture and Philosophy® Series Editor: George A. Reisch

For full details of all Popular Culture and Philosophy® books, visit www.opencourtbooks.com.

Popular Culture and Philosophy®

The Catcher in the Rye and Philosophy

A Book for Bastards, Morons, and Madmen

Edited by
KEITH DROMM
and
HEATHER SALTER

OPEN COURT
Chicago and LaSalle, Illinois

Volume 71 in the series, Popular Culture and Philosophy ®, edited by George A. Reisch

To order books from Open Court, call toll-free 1-800-815-2280, or visit our website at www.opencourtbooks.com.

Open Court Publishing Company is a division of Carus Publishing Company.

Library of Congress Cataloging-in-Publication Data

The catcher in the rye and philosophy : a book for bastards, morons, and madmen / edited by Keith Dromm and Heather Salter.
    p. cm. — (Popular culture and philosophy ; v71)
    Includes bibliographical references and index.
    ISBN 978-0-8126-9800-8 (trade paper : alk. paper)
    1. Salinger, J.D. (Jerome David), 1919-2010. Catcher in the rye.
  2. Philosophy in literature. I. Dromm, Keith. II. Salter, Heather.
    PS3537.A426C3223 2012
    813'.54—dc23

                                          2012027320

Contents

Citations to *The Catcher in the Rye*

References to *The Catcher in the Rye* give the chapter and the page number of the Back Bay Paperback Edition, 2001. For example: "Oh sure! I like somebody to stick to the point and all. But I don't like them to stick *too* much to the point" (24, p. 238). This quote is found in Chapter 24 on page 238 of the Back Bay edition. Since the chapters, but not the page numbers, are the same across the various editions, those who don't have the Back Bay edition will still be able to locate the references pretty quickly.

Are You a Phony?
A Self-Test

Directions: Answer Yes or No to each question. Count the number of times you answer "yes" and then consult the instructions at the bottom to determine your degree of phoniness.

1. Do you like movies? (1, p. 4)
2. Do you smile at but ignore people whom you think are corny? (2, p. 19)
3. Is your name David, Linda, or Marcia? (8, p. 70)
4. Do you smoke a pipe? (8, p. 70)
5. Do you ever give humble bows even though you're a big snob? (12, p. 110)
6. Do you ever use the word "marvelous"? (12, p. 113)
7. Have you ever said "Glad to've met you" to someone you were not glad to have met? (12, p. 114)
8. Do you give innocent smiles when you're really guilty? (13, p. 116)
9. Are you a Disciple? (14, p. 130)
10. Are you a minister? (14, p. 131)
11. Do you use the word "grand"? (15, p. 138)
12. Are you a fan of the Lunts? (16, p. 152)
13. Are you an actor? (16, p. 153)
14. Do you have an Ivy league voice? (17, p. 166)
15. Do you wear a checkered vest? (17, p. 166)
16. Do you ever talk about your car's gas mileage? (17, p. 169)
17. Do you ever talk about plays or books in a loud voice so everyone can hear? (17, p. 169)

18. Are you the protagonist of *A Farewell to Arms*? (18, p. 182)
19. Are you a lawyer? (22, p. 223)
20. Do you not like digressions? (24, p. 238)

How many questions did you answer "yes" to?

16–20   You're a **total phony**

11–15   You're **mostly phony**

5–10   You're **somewhat phony**

0–4   You're **not a phony** (Congratulations, Phoebe!)

All That David Copperfield Kind of Crap

KEITH DROMM and HEATHER SALTER

On January 27th, 2010, J.D. Salinger passed away at the age of ninety-one. Despite Salinger's living in self-enforced "anonymity-obscurity"[1] for most of his life, and so doing little directly to promote it, his most famous novel *The Catcher in the Rye* has remained a bestseller since being published in 1951. This success has been continued by its many translations into other languages.

The contributors to this volume are indicative of the novel's wide and enduring appeal. They come from throughout the United States and Europe, as well as Australia and the Middle East. They are writing about *The Catcher in the Rye*, despite it being the story of an adolescent, from many different stages of life. Some first read it when they were Holden's age; others read it later in life. They all became devoted fans after first reading it.

How can the story of a teenager from an upper-class background, who attends boarding schools in the northeastern United States and makes his home in Manhattan, have such a diverse fan base? Despite the specifics of his biography, Holden's experiences are universal and not ones peculiar to youth. More

---

[1] This is Salinger's own term; it comes from a remark by him on the dust jacket flap of the first edition of his novel *Franny and Zooey* (1961): "It is my rather subversive opinion that a writer's feelings of anonymity-obscurity are the second-most valuable property on loan to him during his working years." He leaves us to infer the first-most important.

than his experiences, Holden's reactions to them resonate with his readers. His detections of *phoniness* in the people and institutions around him, his faltering attempts to share these judgments with others, and the distress all this causes him, are reactions to the world that all fans of his story have had at some point in their lives. For many, they have caused as much trouble—for some even more—as they do for Holden.

Since 1888 We Have Been Molding Boys into Splendid, Clear-thinking Young Men

The adults in Holden's world, like old Spencer or Mr. Antolini, might describe Holden as "confused." This is an apt characterization of him. Holden cannot make sense of society's goals and values. For example, he doesn't understand the importance placed on the outcome of a football game and how "you were supposed to commit suicide or something if old Pencey didn't win" (1, p. 5) or why most people are "crazy about cars" and "worry if they get a little scratch on them" and "always talking about how many miles they get to a gallon" (17, p. 169). His confusion about these things tends to alienate him from his peers and many others. But is Holden's confusion his own fault or society's?

One lesson that the novel might seem to teach, as Louis Menand points out, is that "alienation is just a phase." The confusion of youth eventually gives way to the certainty and confidence of adulthood. *Catcher* has been famously subject to efforts to ban it from school curriculums and libraries ever since its publication. However, despite the obscenities peppered throughout, and Holden's irreverence and frequent flaunting of societal norms, this lesson should actually appeal to those who have tried to ban it. The book, it seems, provides the young people who read it not only some consolation that they're not alone in their confusion, but a vague reassurance that they'll eventually grow out of it. However, as Menand argues, not everyone outgrows Holden's attitude, and they shouldn't, because "it's a fairly useful attitude to have."[2] Many of society's goals and val-

---

[2] Louis Menand, "Holden at Fifty," *The New Yorker*, October 1, 2001; at www.newyorker.com/archive/2001/10/01/011001fa_FACT3?currentPage=all. Accessed July 25, 2011.

ues are phony. The apparent confidence that adults have in them is often just a disguise for their own anxieties and can belie the fact that in their youths they were just as confused as Holden. The real lesson of the novel—at least to many of the contributors to this volume—is that Holden is confused because society doesn't make any sense. In this way, society itself is confused.

Questions Were the Main Thing (Franz Kafka, *The Trial*)

Society is the cause of Holden's confusion, and this causes Holden so much distress because he assumes it should make sense. Holden is a lot like another famous literary figure who went through a "phase" of alienation: Josef K. of Franz Kafka's *The Trial*.

Josef K. is also confused. It begins for him early one morning when he is arrested. The charges against him are never revealed; nevertheless, his trial proceeds slowly over the course of a year. Throughout, the legal process to which he is subjected remains opaque to him; as he remarks: "it's in the nature of this judicial system that one is condemned not only in innocence but also in ignorance."[3] Those around him pretend to have a better understanding of what's happening than he does; they are actually just content with not understanding.

Josef K.'s own lawyer gives him nothing more than "a few empty admonitions, as if talking to a child" and "speeches as useless as they were boring" (p. 112). His lawyer is as helpful as the adults who try to advise Holden. Josef K.'s confusion is not something he can overcome by applying himself, as Mr. Antolini directs Holden to do (24, p. 245), or by playing according to the rules, as old Spencer advises (2, p. 12). Their confusions cannot be cured merely through a change in attitude. The world each character occupies is confused. And those worlds, although exaggerated in some of their details, are supposed to represent our own.

Now, there are better strategies for dealing with our world's confusion than these two protagonists model. Both Josef K. and Holden act recklessly at times. Old Spencer and Mr. Antolini

---

[3] *The Trial*, Schocken, 1998, p. 55.

correctly see the problems with Holden's reactions to the world's confusion and try to point these out to him. Yet, they don't seem to appreciate fully that behind his actions there is a correct view of the world. For one thing, the world *is* filled with phonies.

At any stage in life, reading Holden's story can remind us that the world's confused. Much of our world doesn't make sense, even though most people move through it as though it did and never bother to question it like Holden. To disregard the world's confusion requires sometimes being a phony. While consumed by life's daily tasks, especially those we need to perform to get ahead (or stay afloat) in work or school, we can lose sight of the relative value of these tasks. Holden not only reminds us that winning a football game, having a nice car, and many of society's other goals are of relatively little value; he reminds us of what has most value, our relationships with others. Despite his strained relationships with his roommate, parents, teachers, and others, Holden displays a great concern for the well-being of others. The title of the novel captures this concern, which is revealed in his conversation with the nuns in the diner, his worries over Stradlater's intentions with Jane Gallagher, and even his lies to Mrs. Morrow about her son. But most of all, his devotion to his younger sister Phoebe reveals Holden to be not a self-centered, maladjusted teenager, but someone who cares deeply about others and worries about how the world's confusion can harm them; his love for Phoebe finally calms him and averts, at least for awhile, that "terrible, terrible fall" that Mr. Antolini had warned him about (24, p. 242).

The cause of Holden's confusions, his judgments of phoniness, the advice offered him by old Spencer and Mr. Antolini, and related topics, such as the efforts to ban *Catcher*, are explored in the chapters of this volume. Their authors aim to make some better sense of Holden and his world than he and many of the other characters in *Catcher* are capable of doing. They all agree that there is something right about Holden's view of the world, even though he might falter in some of his judgments and actions.

Our Carrousel Ride

While many books, including other anthologies, have been published on *Catcher*, this volume is unique in using philosophy to sort out Holden's confusion. In doing this, while they provide some facts about Salinger's life, as well as the history and reception of *Catcher*, and they offer unique interpretations of the events in Holden's narrative, our writers are principally concerned with the novel and the philosophical questions it provokes. The philosophical approaches of the authors to these questions are as diverse as their biographies. They draw upon the ideas of philosophers from various periods and movements such as ancient philosophy, existentialism, Christian philosophy, and phenomenology, as well as original philosophical work of their own. Their topics reflect the whole range of philosophical concerns, including metaphysics, ethics, and aesthetics. Many chapters aim to reveal Holden's philosophy; in doing this they offer a glimpse through his "anonymity-obscurity" into some of Salinger's philosophy.

The writers have enjoyed a very special and rare pleasure: to be allowed to combine something at which they make their living (teaching philosophy and other topics) and something that they've been a fan of and has occupied a special place in their lives, the novel *The Catcher in the Rye*. On behalf of all the contributors, we express our gratitude to Open Court, and specifically George Reisch and David Ramsay Steele, for giving us this opportunity. We, the editors, thank the contributors for all their hard work and for enhancing our understanding of *The Catcher in the Rye*. We expect these chapters will do the same for other readers.

We would say more, but you don't want to hear any more of this David Copperfield kind of crap, and besides, when you start telling anybody anything, you begin to start missing everybody.

Lawyers
and
Other
Phonies

1
Mixed Drinks and Mixed Motives

NIC BOMMARITO

As phonies go, few seem as bad as the *moral* phony. Moral phonies go through the motions—they follow the rules, donate to charity, visit sick friends in the hospital—but deep down, they don't really care about what's right. These Lane Coutells[1] might have a variety of reasons for, say, donating to charity: so they'll get a tax write-off, because their accountant said it would be a good idea, in order to get a nice gold plaque. One can discuss their motivation without mentioning anything about what makes giving to charity good.

Those who hate moral phonies may find a friend in Immanuel Kant. If you want to hear the David Copperfield kind of crap, Kant was an eighteenth-century philosopher from the Prussian city of Königsberg. To say he has been influential in modern philosophical thought is an understatement—his ideas are indispensable elements of modern ethics. In the introduction to his moral philosophy *The Groundwork of the Metaphysics of Morals*, Kant emphasizes the role of motivation in our moral evaluations of actions; it's not enough for them to *conform* with morality, they also have to be done *for the sake* of morality. In other words, it isn't enough simply to do the right thing—you have to do it *because it's the right thing*.

To illustrate this, Kant imagines a shopkeeper who doesn't overcharge ignorant customers, but instead he charges every customer the same fair price. However, he doesn't do this

---

[1] A phony in Salinger's novel *Franny and Zooey*.

because he cares about honesty or fairness, but because he knows that a reputation for fairness will be good for business. The shopkeeper acts honestly, but according to Kant, since he is motivated by self-interest rather than concern for what's fair, he gets no moral credit. Moral phonies may *do* the right thing, but they don't deserve any credit for doing it.

For the Love of Dry Martinis

If you thought that Holden Caulfield had nothing in common with eighteenth-century moral philosophers, think about what Holden has to say about lawyers:

> "Lawyers are all right, I guess—but it doesn't appeal to me," I said. "I mean they're all right if they go around saving innocent guys' lives all the time, and like that, but you don't do that kind of stuff if you're a lawyer. All you do is make a lot of dough and play golf and play bridge and buy cars and drink Martinis and look like a hot-shot. And besides. Even if you *did* go around saving guys' lives and all, how would you know if you did it because you really *wanted* to save guys' lives, or because you did it because what you *really* wanted to do was be a terrific lawyer, with everybody slapping you on the back and congratulating you in court when the goddam trial was over, the reporters and everybody, the way it is in the dirty movies? How would you know you weren't being a phony? The trouble is, you *wouldn't.*" (22, pp. 223–24)

Like Kant, Holden points out that we consider a person's motivation when making moral evaluations. After all, the lawyer who's interested only in money and professional respect lacks the moral value we find in a lawyer who cares about justice. When the lawyer motivated by money and prestige saves an innocent guy's life, like Kant's shopkeeper, he does something good only by accident.

Murky Motives

But what about more realistic lawyers motivated by a concern for justice *and* a desire for money? Even though the concern for justice is what's important, would some extra incentive really hurt? Kant seems to think so, because he often writes as if our actions are either done from concern for morality or not, with little room for gray area.

But common sense suggests that people can (and often do!) have mixed motives. Someone can eat broccoli because she likes the taste *and* because she thinks it's healthy. Why should moral actions be any different? One response might be that someone deserves moral praise in proportion to the degree that they're motivated by a concern for what's right. A lawyer who saves an innocent defendant gets moral praise to the extent that a concern for justice did the motivational work.

But Holden suggests a way that adding fast cars and dry martinis to the motivational mix adds special difficulties. Suppose you're the sort of lawyer who's moved by both justice and martinis. Can you really be sure that it's not martinis that get you working on a case? Perhaps that story about justice is just how you reassure yourself on the way to church. Or perhaps concern for justice is what's doing the motivational heavy lifting and concern for professional accolades is merely a result of a compliment-starved childhood. Holden thinks that even *you* wouldn't be able to tell what's doing the motivational work. Once we mix motives, the waters become murky.

Who's the Phony Here?

Whatever the right motivation for saving an innocent guy, in order to know that our lawyer is a moral phony we must know that she doesn't have it (or at least that she has other, less admirable motives that are stronger). Knowing anyone's motives is difficult, even our own. We can't simply ask the lawyer since both the phony lawyer and the good lawyer are apt to claim they're motivated by justice and a concern for life and so on.

The phony doesn't even have to be a liar; she might just get it wrong about why she does what she does. We do this all the time. We spend four years of med school thinking that we love the art of healing, only to realize later how much we were motivated by the need to impress our parents. We swear to our friends that we're going on the camping trip because of our dormant love of the outdoors, when they know that it's because we've fallen for the trip organizer. Conversely, our parents may by convinced that we've taken up the saxophone just because it's popular even though we know that it's because of our deep love of Coltrane's music.

Sometimes we get it wrong about our motives, and sometimes others get it wrong. The lawyer who admits to being a phony who cares only about fast cars and dry martinis may in fact have a deep concern for justice. The lawyer who explains to us in detail how much she cares about justice may do it all simply for an impressive resume. It's very hard to know the motivation behind an action, which makes it very hard to tell who is a phony.

Phoniness and Character

In *The Catcher in the Rye* the word "phony" applies to a lot of things: the word "grand" (2, p. 14) is phony, and bodily gestures like a bow (12, p. 110) or a handshake (7, p. 65) can be phony. But it's not just things or actions that are phony; people themselves are often labeled "phonies." Determining whether or not a person is phony has its own unique difficulties. Suppose we want to know not just whether or not a particular instance of saving an innocent life is phony, but whether or not the lawyer *herself* is a phony.

It might seem as if the lawyer is a phony if her saving the innocent was phony, if she lacked the proper motivation. Let's assume that Mr. Antolini in fact cares very much about Holden and his welfare (he's not simply interested in making sexual advances or other self-serving motives). Now suppose that Mr. Antolini has been sick and having an awful day and late that night Holden calls in search of someone to talk to. Mr. Antolini is too tired and depressed to muster much genuine concern for Holden, but he picks up the phone and does what he can to cheer up Holden and help him feel better. In this instance, Mr. Antolini lacks the motive we think is important for not being a phony, caring feelings for Holden. However, rather than writing off his talking with Holden as phony, one is likely to admire his genuine dedication to Holden. After all, he *usually* cares deeply about him, but is just unable to care *tonight* at three in the morning.

Whether or not his late-night counseling is phony, one bad day is not enough to make *him* a phony. An important feature of calling someone a phony is that she *habitually* lacks the right motivation. One must have information about a person over time—maybe from observing them or talking to those who have known them for a long time—before deciding whether or not he or she is a phony.

These character judgments are made more difficult by the fact that a person's phoniness might only come out in certain circumstances. Sally Hayes might be sincere with her close friends but a phony with strangers. She might try to be sincere with guys she's interested in romantically, but on first dates she's a total phony. When she talks about books she might be very un-phony, but a phony when she talks about theater or movies. It's difficult to notice these patterns and also difficult to decide how much phoniness makes someone a phony.

Phonies in Glass Houses

Not only are the requirements for being a phony hard to identify both in ourselves and in others, but they must be identified over and over if we are to know whether a person is a phony or not. The practical result, given the difficulty of this task and the likelihood of error, is that we should be careful when calling someone a phony as it requires making difficult assumptions about motives which are apt to be colored by our prejudices. This could be as simple as taking a minute to reflect and ask ourselves, "Am I *really* sure this person is doing this just for phony reasons? Why do I think this?" or "Have I really known this person long enough to know if this is part of their character or not?"

This difficulty is at odds with Holden's own behavior in the novel. Holden is astoundingly trigger-happy when it comes to identifying others as phonies: his teacher, Mr. Spencer (2, p. 10); his dorm's namesake, Ossenburger (3, p. 22); an entire crowd smoking outside a play (17, p. 164), to name just a few. Over and over we see Holden make assumptions about why other characters do what they do and then immediately write them off on this basis.

As readers, we also see what this tendency does to Holden. It isolates him and prevents him from connecting to others. Holden himself begins to notice this when he finds himself wondering if maybe he had been wrong in judging Mr. Antolini's motives too hastily (see the start of Chapter 25). For Holden and many teenagers, breaking out of this habit is an important part of growing up. As a reader in high school, I thought I knew exactly what motivated myself and others, and I identified with Holden's criticisms. As I began to question my grasp on the inner workings of people, I came to see my bold Holden-like judgments of phoniness as not only foolish but the source of much unnecessary teenage angst about being oh-so misunderstood.

What If *Everyone* Did That?

Whether or not we can *tell* if someone is a phony, one still might wonder if being a phony itself is wrong. Kant offered a kind of test to see if an action is wrong. If you want to do something, like read a J.D. Salinger novel or tell a lie to get out of trouble, and you want to know if it is morally okay you simply ask yourself, "How would it be if everyone did that?" You imagine everyone reading Salinger novels and things seem pretty good, so reading Salinger novels is morally acceptable. A Kantian would say the action is "universalizable." Now you try to imagine that everyone told lies whenever it got them out of trouble. In that world, lying would be so common that nobody would ever believe anything anyone else told them. But if nobody believes anything, then it's impossible to lie to anyone. That sort of world doesn't even make sense. So, Kant concludes, it is not morally acceptable to lie.

What about being a phony? Being a phony doesn't always seem to be wrong in the way that Kant thinks lying is wrong. For example, Holden calls Sally and her friend phonies for name-dropping people from their past (see Chapter 17). A world where everyone lies would be impossible, but not a world in which everyone name-drops. We can easily imagine that sort of world (we might be living in one). It might make Holden cringe to think of a world where everyone's a phony, but it's not impossible in the way the world where everyone lies is.

Even Kant, who is famously hard-line about lying, allows for us to say false things in the interest of politeness. He says signing a letter "your obedient servant" is okay because nobody believes it (*Metaphysics of Morals* 6:431). If it's not going to fool anyone anyway, then it is universalizable. In this respect Holden is even more hard-line about phonies. He makes no allowance for actors in a play, Sally engaging in polite conversation, or Mr. Spencer laughing at his boss's jokes, even though it's likely that nobody at all would be fooled by these things.

The Importance of Being Phony

Behaving in a phony way cannot only be innocuous, it can sometimes be an essential step in coming to have morally worthwhile motives. Aristotle, in his *Nicomachean Ethics*, emphasizes the role of habituation in becoming virtuous (for example, 1103b). Suppose you reflect on your motives and find that you lack some morally important ones, how might one acquire them? This is a problem most of us face. One common solution is to simply act the part and let the rest come later.

Imagine someone who after talking to a friend he admires, wishes he could develop the same concern for others and generosity that he sees in his friend. He decides to volunteer at the local homeless shelter and though he initially cares little about those he serves, he gradually comes to be motivated by genuine concern for their wellbeing. He was only able to attain this state by being a phony and acting the part of a more moral person.

This is the moral version of going to the museum to get your date to think you have an appreciation for impressionist paintings and after a few hours finding you have actually developed a love of Monet. When you bought your ticket you were a phony playing a part, you thought it would be nice to be care about the paintings but you simply didn't. But by playing the part of someone who cared about such things and acting as they would—by being a phony—you came to actually be the thing you were pretending that you were.

Habituation is difficult and acting the part does not always result in becoming the character we play. But to write off all phoniness, all instances of acting without the proper motivation, is to write off a useful tool in becoming the sort of person we want to be.

We're all full of complicated, changing, and hidden motives. It's hard to know which motives are important, whether or not someone has them, and how deep they run. It's also difficult to know what will be helpful in developing the sort of motives we think are worthwhile. We, like Holden, struggle with varying degrees of success to keep this in mind when sizing up others. And like Holden, when we do manage to keep these difficulties in mind, we can find ourselves missing those we previously wrote off as phonies.[2]

---

[2] My *genuine* thanks to the very un-phony Chris Walsh, Michael Connolly, and Alex King for all their help.

2
The Most Terrific Liar You Ever Saw in Your Life

DON FALLIS

One of the main reasons that Holden Caulfield is the quintessential alienated youth is that so many people seem to him to be phonies. Being a phony involves a certain sort of insincerity. In particular, a phony represents himself as being some thing or some way that he isn't. For example, Holden's roommate at Pencey Prep, old Ward Stradlater, always makes sure that he looks immaculate, but he is really "a secret slob" (4, p. 35).

Given his antipathy toward phoniness, it's ironic (or "ironical" as Holden would put it) how insincere *Holden* himself often is. Holden admits to us (his readers) that he constantly *lies* to other people. In fact, he claims to be "the most terrific liar you ever saw in your life" (3, p. 22). When he meets the mother of a classmate on the train to New York City, Holden begins by lying to her about his name. Then he describes to her in great detail what a good guy her son is despite the fact that he actually thinks that old Ernest Morrow is "the biggest bastard that ever went to Pencey" (8, p. 71).

While Holden is probably doing something wrong when he tells such lies, most readers are inclined to agree with Holden that the insincerity of the phonies is worse. But if this is true, what's the crucial moral difference? We can try to resolve this moral puzzle by appealing to the philosophical work on lying and other forms of insincerity.

Being Altruistic

One difference between Holden and the phonies is that their insincerity is typically self-serving. For example, old Stradlater

11

is a phony precisely because he tries to make himself look better than he really is. Similarly, "the big phony bastard" old Ossenburger (who "gave Pencey a pile of dough") speaks to the school "telling us all about what a swell guy he was" (3, p. 23). By contrast, Holden often has altruistic motives for his insincerity. For example, he lies to old Morrow's mother because he likes her and wants to protect her from the truth about her son.

However, it's not clear that Holden's altruism really gets him off the hook for his lying. The most famous philosopher to discuss lying was Immanuel Kant. And he thought that lying was "the *greatest violation* of a human being's duty to himself regarded merely as a moral being."[1] Kant argued that lying is always wrong, regardless of your motives. It is wrong to lie even if you do so to save someone's life. For example, suppose that a murderer comes to your front door. According to Kant, it would be wrong for you to lie about the whereabouts of her intended victim, even if there's no other way to protect this person.[2]

Most philosophers today think that Kant's position on lying was a bit extreme to say the least. In fact, several have argued that Kant's own moral theory permits you (and may even require you) to lie to bloodthirsty murderers, terrorists, Nazis, headmasters, et cetera. But even though there may be such extreme cases where it's okay to lie, Harvard philosopher Sissela Bok argues that it is almost always wrong to lie even when it's done for the good of others.[3]

The potential harms of lying are so great that they rarely outweigh the expected benefits. For instance, lies have the potential to destroy the trust that we need in order to effectively co-operate and share information with other members of society. If old Morrow's mother ultimately found out that Rudolf Schmidt is a janitor at Pencey and not one of the students, she probably would have been somewhat less inclined to believe what other people say after that. And it's not as if Holden's lie was justified by the fact that lives were at stake.

---

[1] *The Metaphysics of Morals*, Cambridge University Press, 1996, p. 182.

[2] "On a Supposed Right to Lie from Altruistic Motives" in *Critique of Practical Reason and Other Writings in Moral Philosophy*, University of Chicago Press, 1949.

[3] Sissela Bok, *Lying*, Random House, 1978, pp. 32–46

This is not to suggest that Holden should instead have told old Morrow's mother what he really thought of her son. The fact that it's rarely okay to lie does not mean that you should therefore say everything that you believe to be true.[4] Holden probably should have just kept his mouth shut about old Morrow.

Altruism does not excuse all of Holden's lies because he doesn't always lie for the good of others. He tells his history teacher, old Spencer, that "I have to get going now. I have quite a bit of equipment at the gym I have to get to take home with me. I really do" (2, p. 20) just so he can get the hell out of there. In fact, some of his self-serving lies might even harm other people. For example, he regularly tries to convince bartenders that he is over twenty-one so that they will serve him "intoxicating liquor" (10, p. 91) rather than just Coke. But as Holden recognizes, these bartenders could "lose their jobs if they got caught selling to a minor."

Shooting the Bull

Maybe Holden's insincerity is more excusable because he was just *bullshitting* rather than actually lying. According to Princeton philosopher Harry Frankfurt, bullshitting falls "short of lying."[5] Unlike lies, bullshit is "produced without concern with the truth, it need not be false" (pp. 47–48).

In fact, Holden's very explicit about being a bullshitter. He tells us that he was "shooting the bull" (2, p. 18) when he talked to old Spencer. Also, Holden was "chucking the old crap around" (8, p. 73) when he talked to old Morrow's mother. But it's not clear that being a bullshitter really gets Holden off the hook either.

For one thing, the fact that you're bullshitting does not mean that you're not also lying.[6] Frankfurt tends to give the

---

[4] Thomas L. Carson, *Lying and Deception*, Oxford University Press, 2010, pp. 257–266.

[5] *On Bullshit*, Princeton University Press, 2005, p. 19.

[6] See, for example, *Lying and Deception*, pp. 61–62 or G.A. Cohen, "Deeper into Bullshit" in *Bullshit and Philosophy* (Open Court, 2006), pp. 122–29. In fact, Frankfurt himself admits as much in his "Reply to G.A. Cohen" in *Contours of Agency*, MIT Press, 2002. He just claims that bullshitters "are liars only, as it were, incidentally or by accident."

impression that lies and bullshit are mutually exclusive categories. However, your bullshit *is* a lie if you say something that
you believe to be false and you intend to be taken seriously.[7]
And Holden certainly makes many false statements while he's
shooting the bull. For instance, he tells old Morrow's mother
that he's bleeding because he "got hit with a snowball" (8, p. 73)
when, in fact, old Stradlater beat him up.

It might be the case that "bullshit lies" are not as bad as
other sorts of lies. However, Frankfurt argues that it's actually
the other way around. Bullshitting is a worse kind of insincerity than lying in general. The bullshitter will make a statement
"without bothering to take into account at all the question of its
accuracy" (p. 31). And it can be very dangerous for society when
we stop caring about what the facts really are (as seems to be
happening more and more in politics and the media these
days). Thus, Frankfurt claims that "bullshit is a greater enemy
of the truth than lies are" (p. 61).

Being a bullshitter is not actually something that distinguishes Holden from the phonies. Phonies frequently say
things when they have no concern about whether or not what
they're saying is true. Frankfurt describes "a Fourth of July
orator, who goes on bombastically about 'our great and blessed
country, whose Founding Fathers under divine guidance created a new beginning for mankind'" (p. 16). Since the goal of
this bullshit is to get his audience "to think of him as a patriot,
as someone who has deep thoughts and feelings about the origins and the mission of our country," Holden would certainly
consider him to be a phony. Similarly, when old Lillian
Simmons sees Holden at Ernie's night club in Greenwich
Village, she says "how marvelous" (12, p. 113) it is to see him
when all she's really interested in is hearing about his successful brother, D.B. Holden's editorial comment about her bullshit is that she is "strictly a phony." Holden himself is guilty of
exactly the same sort of phoniness. A short while later, he tells

---

[7] When Ackley keeps bothering him while he's trying to read, Holden sarcastically says, "This *sentence* I'm reading is terrific" (3, p. 28). Later, he pulls
his fancy red hunting cap over his eyes and claims to have gone blind. Holden
believes these statements to be false. But they are not lies since they're not
intended to be taken seriously. See my article, "What is Lying?", *Journal of
Philosophy* 106:1 (2009).

us, "I'm always saying 'Glad to've met ya' to somebody I'm not at *all* glad I met."

Using Your Words

Another possible difference is that, while Holden lies with words, phonies typically lie with their actions. For example, old Stradlater doesn't ever say that he's not a slob. In addition, Holden tells us about "a big phony handshake" (7, p. 65), "this very phony, innocent look" (13, p. 116), "those very phony, Ivy League voices" (17, p. 166), old Maurice wearing "a phony shirt collar" (14, p. 133), and "this very phony, *humble* bow" (12, p. 110) that Ernie gives after his performance on the piano.

Admittedly, phoniness often does involve a lot of talking. But even so, the insincerity still has more to do with how phonies *behave* than with any particular thing that they say. Holden reports that, at the intermission of the play starring the Lunts, "you never saw so many phonies in all your life, everybody smoking their ears off and talking about the play so that everybody could hear and know how sharp they were" (17, p. 164).

Mark Twain once claimed that "nonverbal lies" are worse than standard verbal lies. He wrote that

> by examination and mathematical computation I find that the proportion of the spoken lie to the other varieties is as 1 to 22,894. Therefore the spoken lie is of no consequence, and it is not worth while to go around fussing about it and trying to make believe that it is an important matter. ("My First Lie, and How I Got Out of It" in *The Man That Corrupted Hadleyburg*, 1917, p. 169)

But this only suggests that people are more likely to be deceived by nonverbal lies because such lies are more prevalent. The consensus among moral philosophers is that, all other things being equal, telling a verbal lie *is* worse than telling a nonverbal lie. Unlike nonverbal lies, verbal lies involve a *betrayal of trust* (*Lying and Deception*, p. 34). Whenever you make an assertion, you're asking your audience to trust that what you are saying is true. Holden often makes it quite explicit that he's offering his assurance by prefacing his remarks with, "If you want to know the truth." And when you make an assertion that you know to be false, you are violating that trust. Holden assures old Spencer that he has to get to the gym when the facts are otherwise. By contrast, old Stradlater doesn't ask anyone to believe that he's not a slob. He just hopes that they will leap to this conclusion on their own.

But even if Twain were right and nonverbal lies were worse, it would still not get Holden off the hook. Holden himself sometimes tries to deceive without using words. For instance, he does not simply tell bartenders that he's over twenty-one. Among other things, he stands up to order his drinks so that bartenders "could see how tall I was and all and not think I was a goddam minor" (19, p. 185).

Not Lying to Yourself

Everything that we've considered so far actually seems to suggest that Holden's insincerity is as bad, if not worse, than the insincerity of the phonies. In fact, when you get right down to it, it is not even clear that phonies *are* insincere in the first place. They certainly give a false impression about themselves. But phonies tend to believe their own press (old Stradlater and old Ossenburger certainly do). In addition to deceiving others, they deceive themselves. Thus, phonies can actually be quite sincere when they represent themselves as being a certain way.

In fact, phoniness is apparently completely consistent with massive self-deception. When Holden explains to his sister, old Phoebe, why he does not want to become a lawyer like his father, he says:

> even if you *did* go around saving guys' lives and all, how would you know if you did it because you really *wanted* to save guys' lives, or because you did it because what you *really* wanted to do was be a terrific lawyer, with everybody slapping you on the back and congratulating you in court when the goddam trial was over. . . . How would you know you weren't being a phony? The trouble is, you *wouldn't*. (22, pp. 223–24)

Admittedly, Holden himself may be self-deceived to some degree. For instance, his plan to "hitch hike out west" and then "build . . . a little cabin somewhere with the dough I made and live there for the rest of my life" (25, p. 258) seems a bit far-fetched. In addition, he realizes later that he was deceiving himself when he declared his love for old Sally Hayes. Holden tells us, "it was a lie, of course, but the thing is, I *meant* it when I said it" (17, p. 163). But this isn't nearly enough to get him off the hook. Most of the time, Holden knows perfectly well that what he says to other people is false.

Now, while they may not always do so intentionally, it's no accident that phonies give a false impression about themselves. They're like the Pierid butterflies that have evolved to resemble the Heliconid butterflies.[8] Birds find Pierids very tasty, but they get very sick when they eat Heliconids. So, a Pierid can avoid getting eaten if it appears to birds to be an Heliconid. Of course, resembling Heliconids is not something that Pierids do intentionally. It is just that, in the past, Pierids that happened to resemble Heliconids were more likely to survive and to pass on their genes to future generations of Pierids. The deceptive behavior of phonies arguably has a similar *adaptive value*. It leads to success for the phonies that reinforces the deceptive behavior, even if the phonies are not consciously aware of it.

In fact, their deceptive behavior may be even more successful precisely because it deceives the phonies themselves as well as other people. As Friedrich Nietzsche put it, "with all great deceivers there is a noteworthy occurrence to which they owe their power. In the actual act of deception . . . they are overcome by belief in themselves. . . . Self-deception has to exist if a grand effect is to be produced. For men believe in the truth of that which is plainly strongly believed."[9]

But if phonies are not intentionally (or even consciously) giving a false impression, are they really doing anything wrong? After all, it is not as if Pierid butterflies are morally blameworthy for misleading hungry birds. Admittedly, unlike the butterflies, phonies may bear some responsibility for being unaware of what they are doing. For instance, old Stradlater

---

[8] See, for example, David Livingston Smith, *Why We Lie*, St. Martin's Press, 2004, pp. 38–39.

[9] *Human, All Too Human*, Cambridge University Press, 1986, p. 40. Along similar lines, Brian Huss ("Bluffing, Lying, and Bullshitting" in *Poker and Philosophy*, Open Court, 2006, pp. 134–35) suggests that some degree of self-deception might make bluffing in poker more effective.

and old Ossenburger certainly could have tried to be a little more self-critical and to recognize that they were giving people a false impression about themselves. But even if phonies are negligent to some degree, deceiving people *on purpose* as Holden does still seems worse.

Being Authentic

There may yet be something that makes phoniness worse. Phonies do not mislead about just anything. They mislead themselves and other people *about who they are*. They're not being genuine. Unlike Holden, phonies are arguably guilty of what the great Existentialist philosophers Martin Heidegger and Jean-Paul Sartre called *inauthenticity*.

To be authentic is to take responsibility for our own lives rather than mindlessly adopting the norms and roles that society presses on us. But phonies tacitly follow old Spencer's advice that "life *is* a game that one plays by the rules" (2, p. 12). Like Sartre's example of the waiter who is really just "playing at being a waiter in a café" (p. 218), phonies are merely putting on a performance in which they take on a pre-existing role. According to Sartre, human beings "are condemned to be free" (p. 32). But phonies deny their freedom and their ability to choose who they are. Thus, in Sartre's terminology, phonies act in "bad faith" (p. 204).

Admittedly, Holden sometimes misleads other people about who he is. For instance, in addition to pretending to be older than he really is so that bartenders will serve him drinks, he pretends to be the nephew of the Dicksteins who had the other apartment on his floor (21, p. 204) so that the new elevator guy in his building will take him up.[10] But this sort of behavior just makes Holden a *confidence man* of sorts. And while a conman is certainly being insincere when he pretends to be someone that he is not, he is not being inauthentic. The deception is done for a specific purpose and it is done quite consciously. As Sartre pointed out, unlike the person who lies to himself, the self-aware liar is not acting in bad faith since he is not trying

---

[10] With this bit of deceit, Holden may also have been trying to even the score with elevator operators. Earlier on, the elevator guy at the Edmont Hotel had lied to Holden about the price of a prostitute (13, p. 119).

to hide from who he is (p. 207). So, surprisingly enough, the fact that phonies lie to themselves as well as to others (one of the things that seemed to make them morally superior to Holden) is an important part of what makes them inauthentic.

But does their inauthenticity make phonies *morally* bad? Whether or not a person is authentic might seem to be morally irrelevant. For instance, as Charles Guignon points out, it is quite possible to be an authentic bastard instead of a "phony bastard" (3, p. 23). But some degree of authenticity is needed for a person to become "a mature, fully developed moral agent" (p. 286). In particular, the virtue of *integrity* seems to require authenticity.

And notwithstanding his constant lying, Holden has a certain sort of integrity. Holden at least tries to be honest with himself in a way that phonies do not. In addition, Sartre claims that people who are inauthentic lack the virtue of *courage*. He actually calls them "cowards" and "scum" (p. 43). And while Holden admits that he is "one of these very yellow guys" (13, p. 115) in personal interactions, he does not shrink from his freedom to choose who he is. Indeed, his choice to be a rebellious liar might actually make Holden more authentic and, thus, more virtuous than the phonies that annoy him so much.

Admittedly, Holden is just as much of a bullshitter as the phonies. And his deceptions are often just as self-serving. Moreover, the fact that he uses verbal lies and the fact that he rarely deceives himself tend to make his duplicity more objectionable. However, there is a difference between phonies and Holden that explains why phonies are *morally* worse than Holden despite all his lies. Holden is genuine in a way that phonies are not. Thus, we do have good reason to identify with Holden and to criticize phoniness wherever we find it.

Digression!

According to Holden, "the trouble with me is, I *like* it when somebody digresses. It's more *inter*esting and all" (24, p. 238). I am totally on board with this sentiment. In addition to forcing us to confront a difficult *moral* puzzle, Holden's lying raises an interesting *metaphysical* puzzle.

Given that Holden lies to other people so frequently, it would be surprising if he never intentionally said anything false to us, his readers. Indeed, it is somewhat suspicious the number of times that he says to us, "If you want to know the truth." So, for the sake of argument, let's assume that Holden is an "untrustworthy narrator" (like the narrator of Agatha Christie's *The Murder of Roger Ackroyd*, for example).

Now, if the narrator of a story tells us something that he believes to be false, it seems pretty clear that we have been lied to. But who could have done the lying in the case of *The Catcher in the Rye*? Not Holden. Since he is a fictional character, he cannot *actually* do anything. As Princeton philosopher David Lewis would have put it, Holden can only lie *in the fiction*.[11] And presumably, not J.D. Salinger either. He is just telling a story. While writers of fiction certainly make stuff up, they are not lying, strictly speaking.

It might be suggested that we have made a mistake in assuming that we have *actually* been lied to. Just as Holden only lies in the fiction, perhaps we have only been lied to *in the fiction*. However, there are problems with this suggestion. For one thing, it is not immediately clear how *fictional* things can happen to *real* people. Furthermore, it seems pretty clear that something *actually* happened to us. If the narrator of a story says to us something that he believes to be false, we are likely to be deceived. For example, few readers of *The Murder of Roger Ackroyd* realize that the narrator is the murderer until it is revealed by Hercule Poirot at the very end of the novel. And if we are deceived, it is on purpose. Thus, it still looks like the thing that actually happened to us is that we were *lied* to. But if so, *who* lied to us?

My own thought is that, while we may actually have been deceived, we have not actually been lied to. If Holden is an untrustworthy narrator and we are deceived by what he says, it must be *Salinger* who is doing the deceiving. Similarly, Agatha Christie is clearly the one who deceives the readers of *The Murder of Roger Ackroyd*. Now, if he wrote things about his fictional world that he believed to be false and with the intention of deceiving his readers, Salinger *lied* to us according to the definition that philosophers usually give (even if it is Holden who supposedly says these things). For instance, Bok

---

[11] "Truth in Fiction" in *Philosophical Papers*, Volume I, Oxford University Press, 1983.

says, "I shall define as a lie any intentionally deceptive message which is *stated*" (p. 13). But I think that this popular definition of lying is incorrect. As I have argued elsewhere, lying does not actually require intending to deceive.[12] Instead, lying requires intending to violate a norm of conversation against saying things that you believe to be false. And this norm of conversation is clearly not in force when you tell a story. So, Salinger is not a liar even if he deceives us via his untrustworthy narrator Holden.[13]

---

[12] "What Is Lying?", pp. 39–43 and pp. 55–56.

[13] I would like to thank Keith Dromm, Laura Lenhart, S.J. Lenhart, James Mahon, Clancy Martin, Kay Mathiesen, Heather Salter, and Dan Zelinski for many helpful suggestions.

3
Love and Squalor at the Antolinis'

STIJN DE CAUWER

At the end of Chapter 24, Holden Caulfield is having the fright of his life. Deep asleep in the apartment of the Antolinis, he suddenly feels a hand stroking his head. When he jumps up, he sees Mr. Antolini sitting on the ground next to the sofa he was sleeping on, patting his head like a little boy.

What the hell was he doing? Was this old boozer making a pass at him? Holden rushes off to the nearest elevator to get out of there as fast as possible, even though it's the dead of night. He throws out a silly excuse to the baffled Antolini: that he had left a bag somewhere which he immediately has to go pick up. Never had he waited so long for an elevator to arrive, mumbling random nonsense to Antolini who tries to persuade him to stay. "You're a strange boy", he tells Holden. "Yeah right. Strange my ass. Who is acting strange here?", Holden wants to reply, but he keeps his mouth shut, unable to hide his trembling (24, p. 251).

In his rush to get out of there as fast as he can, Holden barely has the time to realize where he is or what had happened the evening before. Weary and tired of all the emotional turmoil of the past days, he had impulsively chosen to visit the apartment of the Antolinis, if not to receive some useful advice, then at least to find a place to crash for the night. It turned out that Mr. Antolini had already received a worried notice from Holden's father, informing him that his son was not doing well in school and seemed to be in an overall confused state. Mr. Antolini had proceeded to give Holden some advice because he was worried that Holden was headed for a terrible fall. Holden was unimpressed by Antolini's advice, barely able to keep his eyes open. All he wanted to do was sleep.

Antolini advised Holden to "apply himself." How should Holden have understood this advice? Was it merely the phony pep-talk that a teacher gives to a schoolboy while patting him on the head that he should do his best and get good marks? Or was it just the generic ramblings of a tipsy old man who was secretly attracted to this handsome young boy? Whatever the advice was, after the nightly events Holden had pushed it even more to the back of his mind, longing to forget the existence of Antolini altogether.

Antolini's advice was certainly a lot more profound than some simple pep-talk. In fact, the nocturnal shock made Antolini's advice all the more relevant. Holden's panic-stricken reaction proves that the advice was necessary. What exactly does it mean for a person to "apply himself"? The French philosopher Michel Foucault has argued that this was the central concern for the Greek philosophers.[1] The imperative that has become the most famous and most commonly associated with classical Greek philosophy is: "Know yourself." In Foucault's view, the imperative "Know yourself" had been detached from another imperative, from which it was inseparable and which was a much more central concern in Greek thought, and this was: "Take care of yourself," or "Apply yourself."

The Confusions of Alcibiades

It takes Foucault an entire course of lectures to unpack this seemingly simple and vague imperative. In them he devotes a lot of attention to a dialogue by Plato called *Alcibiades*. This dialogue is a conversation between the young and ambitious Alcibiades and Socrates.

Holden's confusions are very much like the situation Alcibiades found himself in. Alcibiades was a stunningly beautiful young boy from a wealthy background who in his childhood had the legendary Pericles as his tutor. When he had reached maturity, it was time to take up the responsibilities that his remarkable upbringing and social position demanded

---

[1] Michel Foucault, *The Hermeneutics of the Subject: Lectures at the Collège de France 1981–1982*, Picador, 2006.

of him: he wanted to become a politician, only he had no clue how to do such a thing. He turns with his concerns to Socrates, the most famous of all Athenian philosophers.

Socrates gives young Alcibiades precisely the same advice that Mr. Antolini gives to Holden: that he should apply himself. Just like Alcibiades, Holden is a boy from a privileged background who is supposed to take up a social position his background demands of him, with everything this entails, such as going to college and getting a good degree. Whereas Alcibiades has no idea what he's supposed to do, Holden is strangely disappointed by the trajectory society had laid out for someone like him. Instead of providing him with great insights and revelations, school had left Holden uninspired and empty. Given their situation, what does it mean for these two young men to apply themselves?

Alcibiades seems to have everything going for him. He has been raised by the most prestigious tutors. He grew up in a family of great wealth and good standing, providing him with powerful connections. He is endowed with a beauty that never fails to make the heads of the Athenians spin and has to turn down one after another sexual offer. Relationships between men, and between older men and young boys, were commonly accepted in ancient Greek society and Alcibiades drew the attention of many prominent Athenian men. Still, his near-perfect upbringing has left him utterly unprepared for politics.

Socrates warns him that everything he has ever learned will be of no use if he wants to govern others. What has been lacking is the care of himself; the care of his soul. In this context, the famous imperative "Know yourself" is nothing more than a counsel of prudence: be aware of your own ignorance. Know that all the knowledge you have received so far will be of no use if you have failed to take care of yourself. Alcibiades needs to apply his mind to himself. He needs to learn what he does not know, what his weaknesses are and how to have the right comportment to the problems he will encounter. What he needs is a skill set or know-how, but the Greek view differs from later philosophical thought in that this know-how is not just a form of received knowledge; it requires first and foremost a transformation of the self.

According to Foucault, the Greek coupling of a knowledge of the self with a necessary care of the self has been severed by later philosophers. He discerns what he calls a "Cartesian moment" from which point on it was no longer a precondition for acquiring knowledge to undergo a transformation or to work on yourself. All weight had been shifted to the acquiring of knowledge as such, which from that moment on could be done by a stable and unchanging subject. This removal of the spiritual care of the self was not total, and occasional traces of the view that first a profound transformation of yourself is needed can still be found in philosophy.

The Sense and Non-sense of Education

Holden's crisis began when he ran away from school in complete disappointment. Anyone who has been to college surely felt similar disappointment at some point. Professors who talk with grinding nasal monotone voices and who sap any trace of enthusiasm or inspiration out of your body. Classes that appear to go on infinitely, with a mind-numbing subject matter of which no one has a clue why it would be relevant to anyone, let alone to their studies. Dull teachers who seem to lack all basic human capacity to explain a simple idea or relate to the human beings in front of them. For Holden, this was Mr. Vinson, whose class in Oral Expression he had flunked.

The English literature classes were all right, but that goddam Mr. Vinson and his Oral Expression class made no sense to him. The class consisted of students who had to give a talk about a topic in front of the class, and every time they strayed from the topic, the entire class had to yell: "Digression!" It drove Holden crazy.

One day, it was the turn of this shy kid, Richard Kinsella, who told the class with trembling lips about his father's farm in Vermont. He kept on digressing to topics that in Holden's view were much more interesting than his father's farm, but the students kept yelling "Digression!" and the kid got a D plus. Holden was just revolted by this. The boy wanted to talk about things that he actually found interesting and that made him excited, but the pitiless students kept on punishing him for it. What in heaven's sake is wrong with something that you find interesting and exciting? Holden thought that his speech was far more interesting than all the others. What in the world is inspiring about sticking to a dull topic, which had to be so mundane in the first place that you could talk about it in such an oversimplified manner anyway? Was this class some kind of a drill in trying to be as boring as possible? Was it meant to kill the last spark of enthusiasm in a person?

Mr. Antolini tries to defend the class by saying that surely there is a right time and place for everything and that you should stick to your guns while trying to get something across. But still, Holden was appalled by that idiot Vinson and his irritating exercise. He refused to play along and got an F. What was the point of this class: trying to keep your ramblings as dull and robotic as possible? This can't be the point of "oral expression." The class reduced oral expression to mere rhetoric without any concern for what mattered.

In ancient Greece the enemy of the Greek philosophers were the rhetoricians. For sums of money, they would teach young Athenians how to sound sophisticated, how to win arguments and outdo your opponent with pure rhetorical skill. The students of rhetoric were taught how to embellish themselves, such as adorning their hair and clothes, in order to enhance the power of their vacant persuasive statements. It was simply training in how to be phony. Socrates reproached these teachers of rhetoric for never having any concern whatsoever for the truth, the good, or their souls.

When Richard Kinsella digressed, there was finally a trace of soul. Something actually *mattered* to the boy and he wanted to share it. The knowledge Holden gets exposed to in school leaves him cold. It doesn't move him nor does it fire up any enthusiasm. In fact, it makes him nauseous and gives him a headache. Mr. Antolini is worried that Holden will generalize his bad experience and dismiss education as a whole. He's afraid that Holden might turn out to be one of those embittered adults who sits in a bar, hating anyone who looks like he could have been a football jock in college, wasting his days on some dull and unstimulating office job. The worst thing that could possibly happen is that a person gives up searching. In the words of Antolini, Holden could become one of those persons who

were looking for something their own environment couldn't supply them with. Or they thought that their own environment couldn't supply them with. So they gave up looking. They gave up before they even started. (24, pp. 243–44)

This state is what the Greeks called a state of irresoluteness. A person who is irresolute will float through his or her life, experiencing both the self and the world as a vague, confusing mess, and eventually will succumb to the confusion and stop seeking. The first thing that such a person had to do was to *will the self.* The person needed to make something of himself, to take care of himself. He needs to establish himself as a subject who is capable of facing the turbulence of life.

The Greeks had a particular word for the skills you had to learn, and that is *paraskheuè.* What form of knowledge was this *paraskheuè* that an irresolute person had to learn? It has to be distinguished from the scholarly knowledge that you learn in order to function in a certain profession. This is the type of knowledge which bores Holden in school. *Paraskheuè* is translated in English as equipment, or tool-kit. This knowledge is not a set of ideas or information, but a series of skills which you could be trained in and that makes you able to face unexpected challenges and problems in life.

It's a form of armature or a tool-box of mental skills to deal with unexpected events. This is exactly what Holden's high school education failed to provide, and it's precisely what the Greek philosophers meant by "care of the self." It's not some kind of a selfish self-styling that turns one into an arrogant intellectual dandy, but it is the knowledge required to deal with the self, the others and the world. It's a set of practices, exercises, or techniques (Foucault uses the expression "technologies of the self") which can transform a person into someone who is capable of responding adequately to his or her environment.

With the proper attitude, Holden could have an entirely different experience of academia. As Mr. Antolini tries to tell him, he could learn that there have been many people who felt exactly like him, who experienced a similar crisis and disappointment in life, and moreover, who were capable of expressing their experiences in powerful, inspirational texts. This is not dead knowledge, but a poetic gift that can change your life. People inspired by these records might one day be capable of recording their own story, which in turn will inspire new readers. Holden seems to have taken up Antolini's suggestion because the book we're reading is precisely such a gift; it is Holden's account of his spiritual crisis.

Besides giving you access to inspirational sources, entering academic life with the proper attitude will also provide you with important knowledge about yourself. It will tell you what types of knowledge suit you and which do not. In the words of Antolini:

> it'll begin to give you an idea what size mind you have. What it'll fit and, maybe, what it won't. After a while, you'll have an idea what kind of thoughts your particular size mind should be wearing. For one thing, it may save you an extraordinary amount of time trying on ideas that don't suit you, aren't becoming to you. You'll begin to know your true measurements and dress your mind accordingly. (p. 197)

This passage illustrates perfectly the inseparable connection—central to Foucault's reading of the Greeks—between "to care for yourself" and "to know yourself." It's only after you have begun to take care of yourself, to transform yourself into a subject equipped with the proper attitude and skills that you can begin to know yourself, to know "what size mind you have". Knowledge will remain a dead letter if you have not cultivated the proper attitude to be able to render this knowledge into something fruitful.

Living the Humble Life

In the midst of all this advice which Mr. Antolini gives to the exhausted Holden, and which could have been the advice offered by Socrates wandering the streets of Athens, Antolini chose to give Holden a seemingly un-Greek quote. Antolini finds this quote so important that he had bothered to write it down on a piece of paper. It comes from the now somewhat forgotten psychoanalyst Wilhelm Stekel, a close friend and follower of Freud. The quote goes:

> The mark of an immature man is that he wants to die nobly for a cause, while the mark of the mature man is that he wants to live humbly for one. (p. 195)

This statement seems to be in direct opposition to the attitude of the Greeks. Didn't Socrates give the world a famous example of the opposite by voluntarily drinking the poison cup he was condemned to drink? And what about Alcibiades? When he first meets Socrates, the latter asks him what he would choose if he could either live the way he does now without any glory, or die right now. Alcibidiades answers him firmly that he would rather die on the spot instead of living on without glory (p. 32). Isn't this a blatant contradiction with Antolini's advice to live humbly for a cause instead of dying for one? The kind of cause, and what is meant by "glory" is crucial to understanding the quotation.

Antolini wants to warn Holden against dying for an unworthy cause. He's afraid Holden might fall out of complete disgust for everything around him and drown everything in his confusion, without having developed the proper attitude to face life. What Socrates calls "glory" is not fortune and fame, two things he couldn't care less for, but the development of your soul and living truthfully. If it's unavoidable, Socrates would not hesitate to end his life, but only if the cause is worthy. Socrates too preferred to live humbly, never bothering to write down his philosophy in books that could increase his fame, but to live in accordance with his beliefs on a humble day-to-day basis.

But when we look at Salinger himself, the Stekel advice gets another resonance. The statement has turned out to be prophetic for the unusual life course Salinger was going to take. Having grown up in a generation for which the ultimate glory was to fight for your country in an overseas war, Salinger himself took his life in a completely different direction. His writings became increasingly critical of the detrimental effects war has on a person, something he knew from his own experience, and that the glory to be derived from it was rather dubious. We see this, for example, in the stories, "A Perfect Day for Bananafish" and "For Esmé—with Love and Squalor."

Salinger had most certainly seen his share of action in World War II: he took part in the landing on Utah Beach during D-Day, was part of the liberation of Paris, fought in the fierce Battle of the Bulge and was one of the first soldiers to walk into the camp Dachau during its liberation. After the war, Salinger was hospitalized for so called "combat stress reaction." Everything Salinger had seen and experienced had gotten to him, and traumatized soldiers would regularly appear in his writings. No longer believing in the heroics of war, Salinger's interests turned to the modesty of Buddhism. At the time when

Salinger included the Stekel quote in his book, he couldn't have foreseen what an immense success the novel was going to be, and what fame it would bring him. The novel quickly became a personal favorite of many readers, and Salinger made it to the cover of *Time* magazine.

For most people such a hit would be the equivalent of winning the lottery, but not for Salinger. He detested the immense public attention that the novel had brought him. Still sporadically releasing material for about a decade, he finally had enough and gradually withdrew into his quiet life in the woods of Cornish, New Hampshire, far away from journalists and photographers. He would continue to write, but no longer for a public. He preferred to live a humble life instead of being a celebrated, successful author. It was as if Salinger followed Antolini's advice.

What Makes a Good Teacher?

In the classical Greek view, it's not possible for an individual, on his own strength, to rise above his ignorance and confusion. Only a teacher can help a person to move beyond his or her shortcomings. What makes a good teacher, and what does not, is a very important question to the Greeks. A common view today of a good teacher is someone who provides the pupils with a certain type of knowledge. This is precisely what the Greeks *don't* have in mind. The Mr. Vinson-type professor, doing his thing in front of the pupils, whether they relate to it or not, is not what the Greeks had in mind with a good instructor.

A good instructor is someone who offers a hand: someone who's capable of pulling the pupil out of his current and inadequate comportment to both himself and the world. A successful educator is capable of lifting a student to a new and better way of being, involving a complete change of the pupil. The mere receiving of knowledge is not overcoming your ignorance. A complete transformation of the self is needed. The pupil does not have to amass knowledge, but has to constitute himself as a subject, equipped with a skill set to face potential challenges.

Foucault explains that the activity of the teacher has to be distinguished from the practices of the doctor, the head of the household, and the lover. The doctor who prescribes medicine when a patient is ill only attends to the patient's body, but does not help the patient to transform into someone who can attend to himself, to take care of his soul. The head of the household will take care of the material needs of his family, property and wealth, but not provide the means to take care of his soul. Finally, and especially relevant to Alcibiades and Holden, a teacher should also be distinguished from the care provided by a lover. A lover will only care for a young boy, and more precisely his body, as long as that boy is in his youthful splendor. But when the boy grows up and his exquisite youthful splendor declines, the lover loses interest.

Alcibiades has suitors by the dozens, yet none of them truly cares for Alcibiades's soul. An exception among these suitors is Socrates, and Alcibiades senses this. Socrates is one of the few who can withhold his attraction to the powerful lure of the young boy's ravishing features. Socrates does not approach Alcibiades in order to abandon him as soon as his beauty withers, but because he cares for the soul of Alcibiades. As Foucault puts it: "More precisely, Socrates cares about the way in which Alcibiades will be concerned about himself" (p. 58).

This issue is precisely what is at stake in the night-time events that make Holden rush out of the apartment in panic. He had always thought of Mr. Antolini as a sophisticated and witty intellectual, someone he intuitively turns to in his days of roaming through New York, confused and exhausted. This man, whom he had always respected, turned out to be leaning over him at night like some drunken creep. How should he think of Antolini now? Handsome young boy as he is, Holden claims that such a thing had happened to him several times before: "That kind of stuff's happened to me about twenty times since I was a kid. I can't stand it" (25, p. 251). While young Alcibiades arrogantly turns down all his suitors one by one, not without a slight feeling of satisfaction, Holden reacts to them by running away in total panic: "Boy, I was shaking like a madman. I was sweating, too. When something perverty like that happens, I start sweating like a bastard" (25, p. 251).

This unexpected turn of events has a profound impact on Holden's relation to Antolini as a teacher from whom he would accept important advice. All he wanted to do was to forget about the creep. He wanted to rush away from his fancy apartment as fast as he could, hoping that the speed by which he was getting away from there would erase the entire memory of

Antolini altogether and the fact that Holden went to seek him out. It seems that at this point, Antolini's advice was simply lost on Holden. He had turned out to be one of those people who's only interested in his young body and not in his well-being. He had turned out to be like the many suitors of Alcibiades, only interested in his stunningly beautiful body, and not in the care of his soul. Or at least, this was what Holden had hastily concluded. "One of those", is the quick conclusion he makes before rushing out of the place.

The Letter

Was he right to draw such a conclusion? Antolini had told him the night before that he couldn't express himself at the moment, probably due to the highballs he kept on drinking, but that he was going to send Holden a letter in which he would express himself more eloquently. At that point, Holden assured him that he would certainly read such a letter. Why wouldn't he? He clearly respected and appreciated Antolini's wise suggestions. But would Holden still read that letter after what happened that night? Would he even open the letter when he received it, or simply toss it away in disgust after he had read the name of the sender?

"I'm only sitting here, admiring", is what Antolini told him that night. *Admiring*? Was he admiring this beautiful young boy, whose body he fancied while stroking his hair in the middle of the night, under the influence of alcohol, or was he admiring the complexities of Holden, this tormented young adult who was experiencing an existential crisis about his life? Feeling a deep dissatisfaction with humanity and society at some point in one's life happens to the best and most sincere minds. The ambiguity of what happened that night in Antolini's apartment is in fact even more complex than I have presented it here.

It would be a mistake to see Socrates as some kind of a holier-than-the-pope figure, only concerned with the high and lofty concerns of the soul and completely indifferent to the powerful lust that makes the admirers of Alcibiades lose their minds. Socrates is by no means free from the lure of a young boy's attractive body. In Plato's text Socrates is just as much a suitor of Alcibiades, like all the others fishing for his love.

Where he differs from all the others, is that his attraction would not end when Alcibiades loses the splendor of his youth. Socrates is attracted to the boy's body *and* soul, and he desires that the boy make the best of himself. He would not abandon the boy once he had his way and after the intoxicated lusty haze had passed away.

Socrates was certainly not the only philosopher who appreciated the beauty of boys. In 1958, in a bold act of entrapment, the Polish police sent a young boy to Foucault, who was a visiting scholar there, with the aim of seducing the subversive professor in order to discredit him. Foucault walked right into the trap and had to leave the country or else go to prison.

Similarly, the irritation that Holden feels every time an older man makes a pass at him is also wrapped in ambiguity. Throughout *The Catcher in the Rye*, suggestions are made that Holden had developed some strong bonds with fellow students, bonds that might be a bit more than mere camaraderie. Some readers have read in Holden's fierce reaction to Antolini, who, as far as we know, is doing nothing more than sitting by Holden's side and stroking his hair, a reaction against the feelings towards some fellow students that had been growing in him. It could be that Holden developed a strong affection, more than mere friendship, for some of his friends without really acknowledging it.

The question is not whether Antolini is either a responsible professor giving Holden some unconditional help and advice, or a selfish drunken old man who is simply interested in Holden's handsome body. The possibility also exists that Antolini is both in deep admiration for Holden's physical beauty and charm, but that he can perfectly well keep it in check, while at the same time genuinely wanting the best for Holden and being honestly concerned for his well-being.

The great power of this scene in the story is its multi-faceted moral ambiguity, which creates a tension left unresolved, driving Holden on to new wanderings and encounters. In a sense, Antolini gives Holden a Greek test that night. Did Holden possess the proper attitude, the mental equipment, to face unexpected challenges of life? Or would he simply go in a panic, and run to the nearest exit without thinking or taking up the challenge?

Holden was still unprepared for such a challenge. He had not undergone the transformation that could help him respond adequately to unexpected and complicated difficulties. In his state of mind, any complication is simply one too many. He is already at rock-bottom and does not need more problems.

Applying Himself After All

On the last page of the novel, Holden suggests that he is going to give school another try. Those enigmatic and simple-sounding two words, "Apply yourself," return once again when the psychoanalyst he has been seeing asks him once more: "Are you going to apply yourself?"

Holden still finds it a stupid question. How does he know what he is going to do? He will see what happens when the moment comes. Holden still hasn't entirely come to terms with his irresolution and this two-word imperative, "Apply yourself."

Yet, at the same time, it seems that Holden has made a start with working on himself and turning into someone who's better prepared for the complications of life. He finally goes home to his parents, goes into therapy and is getting ready to give school another try. However briefly suggested on the very last page of the novel, it seems that Antolini's advice to apply himself, which was such a central concern for both the old Greek philosophers and the late Foucault, might have found a fertile ground in Holden after all, even though Holden consciously still resisted it.

4
You Can't Teach Somebody How to *Really* Dance

RICK MAYOCK

It's not surprising that a bright young man with a non-conformist attitude should develop an ironic sense of humor. And it's not surprising that he finds himself in a crisis. On the surface, Holden Caulfield's narration can be read as a series of sarcastic observations revealing a lack of empathy for the characters he encounters and the world in which he finds himself. A closer reading, however, invites us to be included, indirectly, in a deeper ironic interpretation.

According to the philosopher Søren Kierkegaard (1813–1855), indirect, specifically ironic language, opens up a division between those who naively take what is said at face value and those who are perceptive enough to get what is really meant. The careful reader can take pleasure, at least in part, in being in the know and included in the joke.

According to Kierkegaard, irony is a transition phase between what he calls the *aesthetic* and *ethical* spheres of life, and an important means of developing self-understanding and maturation.[1] Holden is caught in the aesthetic stage, living for the pleasure of the moment, and unwilling to take responsibility for his failing grades, or for losing his fencing team's equipment, yet maintaining an attitude of superiority towards his classmates. Yet he has ethical tendencies, exhibited in his compassion for his sister Phoebe, his dead brother Allie, and his fantasy of being a savior of children as "the catcher in the rye."

---

[1] Kierkegaard presents the aesthetic and ethical stages of life in his book *Either/Or*, Princeton University Press, 1987.

These tendencies and his attempts to formulate a social morality despite his sexual urges begin to usher him into what Kierkegaard calls the ethical realm.

Holden finds himself in an existential crisis which has him vacillating between an irresponsible adolescence and a difficult process of growing up. By looking at Holden's struggle through the eyes of Kierkegaard, we can understand him as a character in transition, whose very life is an expression of irony. The use of irony in Holden's narration enables us to recognize the phoniness and inauthenticity that surrounds us, awakens in us a willingness to be included in his inner thoughts, and prepares us to make that awareness part of our subjective experience.

I Can Be Quite Sarcastic when I'm in the Mood

Holden Caulfield practices a kind of *indirect communication* in his narration. He often says one thing yet means another, either by directly letting us know or by indirectly implying that we are included as part of his inner circle. We, the readers, are initiated, right from the outset of the novel, and, if we "really want to hear about it," Holden tells us that he's not going to go into "all that David Copperfield kind of crap." We find out about his past only indirectly through his narrative digressions.

What he's about to reveal to us, if we choose to be initiated, will be shocking and unedited, the uncensored thought processes of an adolescent mind struggling to come to terms with what he perceives to be an inauthentic and phony cultural milieu and set of social conventions.

As readers we have a choice: we can either be put off by the shock value of Holden's language and be, like Holden's parents, "quite touchy" about his personal revelations, or we can accept the invitation and become Holden's confidantes. In order to do so, we need to become aware of what Kierkegaard means by the value of indirect communication. Kierkegaard's writing style is designed to undermine our habitual and static modes of thinking in hopes of forcing us to come up with fresher personal interpretations. The most important means of indirect communication for Kierkegaard is irony, which reveals a disparity between speaking and meaning, or between phenomenon and essence.[2] Literal truth assumes an identity of words and meaning. Ironists, on the other hand don't pretend that what's said is what's meant and maintain a sense of freedom about what they say. They also don't assume or insist that their listeners are aware that they are speaking with irony.

The speaker using irony looks down on those who are not perceptive enough or aware enough to stay with his or her thoughts. Holden's conversation with his former history teacher illustrates this condescension towards those left outside of his thought process. While visiting with "old Spencer" Holden is thinking about the ducks in the lagoon in Central Park:

> I'm lucky, though. I mean I could shoot the old bull to old Spencer and think about those ducks at the same time. It's funny. You don't have to think too hard when you talk to a teacher. (2, p. 18)

Through irony we, the readers, are invited to share in the humor of the situation. We're given the inside information that makes us Holden's accomplices and privy to his thought processes. "All you have to do is say something nobody understands and they'll do practically anything you want them to," he says after lying to the elevator man at his parent's building (21, p. 205). By identifying with Holden's relative charm and sarcasm, we're continually reassured of our inclusion, as long as we get the joke. Understanding ironic speech, according to Kierkegaard, is similar to possessing a riddle and its solution simultaneously.

In general, the use of irony involves distancing oneself from what one is saying. It also liberates the speaker in the sense that the ironist practices a kind of disengagement and is not responsible for the hearer's expectations. This occurs when Ackley hovers over him, blocking the light and doesn't take the hint that Holden is more interested in reading his book:

---

2 Kierkegaard writes: "Already here we have a quality that permeates all irony—namely, that the phenomenon is not the essence but the opposite of the essence. When I am speaking, the thought, the meaning, is the essence, and the word is the phenomenon" (*The Concept of Irony*, Princeton University Press, 1989, p. 247).

> He shoved my book back with his hand so that he could see the name of it. "Any good?" he said.
> "This *sen*tence I'm reading is terrific." I can be quite sarcastic when I'm in the mood. He didn't get it, though. (3, p. 28)

Holden's sarcasm reveals itself as an attitude of superiority and condescension in his attempt to have a conversation with Bernice, the girl he thinks is a good dancer at the Lavender Room:

> "You're a very good conversationalist," I told her. "You know that?"
> "What?"
> I let it drop. It was over her head, anyway. (10, p. 94)

Holden doesn't always expect to be understood by others.

One of Kierkegaard's methods of indirect communication is his use of pseudonyms, which keeps the readers off guard and prevents them from forming static opinions. These different "authors" allow Kierkegaard to assume distinct, often contradictory, voices in order to keep the readers guessing as to which voice is really speaking the truth. This technique enables Kierkegaard to discourage attempts to regard him as the authority or as having the final say on philosophical matters. It allows him to make a fresh start with each new voice and gain a subjective ironic freedom.

Holden often begins a new encounter in an ironic way by using false identities and exercising a subjective freedom which offers the possibility of a new beginning. He's "Rudolph Schmidt" to Mrs. Morrow, the woman he meets on the train to New York, and "Jim Steele" to the girls he meets at the Lavender Room at the Edmont Hotel and to the prostitute Sunny. Holden even agrees to write an essay for Stradlater, copying the poems written on his brother Allie's baseball mitt. "It was very ironical. It really was. '*I'm* the one that's flunking out of the goddam place, and *you're* asking me to write you a goddam composition,'" he says to Stradlater (4, p. 37). Holden's use of false identities enables him to remain in the aesthetic stage and to live in the realm of narrative possibilities.

It Keeps Me from Getting Bored or Something

When Holden becomes a victim of misfortune he expresses very little moral outrage or resentment. On the contrary, after his fight with Stradlater he retreats into Ackley's room and fantasizes about becoming a monk:

> "Listen. What's the routine on joining a monastery?" I asked him. I was sort of toying with the idea of joining one. "Do you have to be a Catholic and all?"
>
> "Certainly you have to be a Catholic. You bastard, did you have to wake me just to ask me a dumb quest—"
>
> "Aah, go back to sleep. I'd probably join one with the wrong kind of monks in it. All stupid bastards. Or just bastards." (7, p. 65)

After his encounter with Maurice, the elevator guy, he again retreats into fantasy, imagining he has been shot in the guts rather than dwelling on the injustice of Maurice's actions.

Kierkegaard describes the aesthetic stage as pre-ethical, not specifically immoral but rather amoral. In the aesthetic evaluation of life, notions of right and wrong take a back seat to immediate sensuous experience. Those in the aesthetic stage are not sufficiently detached from their given circumstances for the notion of responsibility for their existence to arise. Happiness is perceived as the product of good fortune, and unhappiness is the product of misfortune. Holden seems to be in the aesthetic stage when he thinks of losing fights and his "yellowness" as his misfortune or bad luck. It doesn't occur to him that he may have made some bad choices in his dealings with Stradlater or Maurice.

The primary motive for the aesthetic way of life is to transform the boring into the interesting. The aesthetic personality is quite creative in generating intriguing scenarios which involve manipulating people and situations, even creating a false identity. But the aesthetic person lives only in the realm of the possible rather than the actual. When Holden fantasizes, he dwells in the world of the possible, but not for long. As an aesthetic person he only toys with ideas but lacks the capacity to commit to any enduring plan of action.

Holden's use of sarcasm, saying the opposite of what is meant, is also motivated by his need to alleviate boredom. He vents his sarcasm on Ackley (who does not appreciate it) by telling him that Stradlater thinks highly of him. Ackley is more likely to take Holden's comments literally:

> "He's crazy about *you*. He told me he thinks you're a goddam prince," I said. I call people a "prince" quite often when I'm horsing around. It keeps me from getting bored or something. (2, p. 31)

The aesthetic person, according to Kierkegaard, is on a desperate quest for enjoyment, but is ultimately unhappy and self-alienated. Holden has a sense of hopelessness about his interest in Jane Gallagher, and feels he is no real competition for Stradlater:

> I sat there for about a half hour after he left. I mean I just sat in my chair, not doing anything. I kept thinking about Jane, and about Stradlater having a date with her and all. It made me so nervous I nearly went crazy. I already told you what a sexy bastard Stradlater was. (4, pp. 44–45)

According to one of Kierkegaard's pseudononymous authors, Judge William, the aesthetic person misses the possibility of becoming a real person by choosing despair. Holden's fantasy about going off to Massachusetts or Vermont with Sally Hayes also ends in despair. She tells him he should finish school first and then there would be plenty of opportunities for them to travel:

> "No, there wouldn't be. There wouldn't be oodles of places to go to at all. It'd be entirely different," I said. I was getting depressed as hell again. (17, p. 172)

In Kierkegaard's book *Either/Or* the aesthetic person is portrayed by another pseudonym, "A," who scornfully rejects the bourgeois, passionless manner of life, but succumbs to meaninglessness and despair. When "A" meets with failure he sees it not as the result of poor choices, but rather as evidence that no life can be meaningful.

Holden reacts like someone in the aesthetic stage when he fails to assume responsibility for the way his life is going. But there seems to be more to Holden than the urge to satisfy immediate desires. His character is more complex and not limited to the aesthetic way of life. More likely, he is in a transition to the ethical stage. Holden recognizes that he is in some kind of transition during his visit to the museum: "The best thing, though, in that museum was that everything always stayed right where it was. . . . The only thing that would be different would be *you*" (16, p. 158).

The Trouble with Me Is, I *Like* It when Somebody Digresses

In his discussion with Mr. Antolini, Holden mentions that he flunked his class in Oral Expression:

> It's this course where each boy in the class has to get up in class and make a speech. You know. Spontaneous and all. And if the boy digresses at all, you're supposed to yell "Digression!" at him as fast as you can. It just about drove me crazy. I got an *F* in it.

Holden continues: "That digression business got on my nerves. I don't know. The trouble with me is, I *like* it when somebody digresses. It's more interesting and all." He then tells Mr. Antolini: "I like somebody to stick to the point and all. But I don't like them to stick *too* much to the point. I don't know. I guess I don't like it when somebody sticks to the point *all* the time" (24, p. 238).

Sticking to the point is an act of direct communication, which Holden finds to be conventional and boring. Digressing, or going off the point, is indirect communication and is a more sophisticated and, in Kierkegaard's view, a more interesting and valuable means of communication. The best part of the novel is the digressions, when Holden goes off and doesn't stick to the point. The action and dialogue are not as interesting as some of his digressions. If Holden showed no interest in digressions he would be more likely to concern himself with the immediate, and would probably never leave the aesthetic realm. To go off the point is to exercise irony which allows for transition. We learn more about Holden when he goes off the point. As a transition zone, irony opens up the space for reflection. This type of irony allows for moral thinking, focus, and perspective.

Holden's whole life appears to be in transition. Although his gray hair over half of his head gives him the appearance of being older than he is, he's not comfortable as an adult and certainly not comfortable as an adolescent. On the one hand he lives in the aesthetic realm of immediacy with his irresponsible nature and accompanying despair. But on the other hand he has glimpses of the ethical life and struggles to formulate a workable code of ethics.

This struggle is revealed in many ways, including his concern for his sister Phoebe, his reverence for his dead brother Allie, his interest in the children at the museum, his abhorrence of the obscenities written on the school walls, and his fantasy of saving children in danger as the catcher in the rye. Holden's attempts to articulate a sexual morality also indicate he's transitioning from the aesthetic to the ethical realm: "I keep making up these sex rules for myself, and then I break them right away" (9, p. 82). As the novel progresses he evolves from a completely nihilistic and sarcastic attitude about his social existence to a more mature outlook.

Irony is a transition phase, what Kierkegaard calls a *"confinium,"* or border area between the aesthetic and the ethical stages of life.[3] It functions as a midwife at the birth of individual subjectivity, and as a distancing device by creating a space for self-reflection, giving us a sense of perspective. Irony thus enables us to make the transition from the aesthetic way of life to the ethical by acknowledging a longing for something more. It makes ethical reflection possible by freeing us from the limitations of constantly reacting to the immediate. It opens up the focus from what is merely actual to what is possible, from the finite to the infinite, from the particular to the universal.

Holden's fantasy about running away and pretending he's a deaf-mute is an example of indirect communication taken to its extreme—no communication. "That way I wouldn't have to have any goddam stupid useless conversations with anybody" (25, p. 257). But in the process he has a realization that pretending to be a deaf-mute is unrealistic: "I know the part about pretending I was a deaf-mute was crazy, but I liked thinking about it anyway" (25, p. 258). Getting excited about running off reminds him of his responsibility to his sister and his sense of

---

[3] *The Concept of Irony*, p. 121.

commitment. He now appears to be ready to think more maturely and ethically. He motivates himself to communicate with Phoebe, to give her back her money that he borrowed, and to say goodbye. Irony opens the space for ethical reflection, and motivates him to make a choice.

You Know What I'd Like to Be? I Mean if I Had My Goddam Choice?

Holden gives his first indication that he has not quite reached the ethical stage in his conversation with his history teacher, old Spencer:

> "Do you feel absolutely no concern for your future, boy?" old Spencer asks him. "Oh, I feel some concern for my future, all right. Sure. Sure I do." I thought about it for a minute. "But not too much, I guess. Not too much, I guess." (2, p. 20)

Old Spencer sounds here a lot like Judge William (the pseudonym Kierkegaard uses to criticize the aesthetic stage). In order to enter the ethical stage of life, according to Judge William, one needs to make commitments and assume responsibilities.

The aesthetic person is indifferent to time and, like Holden, has trouble developing a consistent character or point of view that persists through time. Ethical choices, for Kierkegaard, require making a vow or contract that defines your character for the future. In order to enter the ethical realm you must develop a self with a personality that is continuous through time and make choices that include future considerations. According to Judge William, vocation and marriage are paradigms for the ethical life because they entail commitments to a lifestyle. The aesthetic person, on the contrary, is only concerned with the immediate satisfaction of desires.

Holden's encounter with the nuns in the little sandwich bar illustrates his struggle to define a ripening moral sense. Their appearance induces Holden to reflect on his unformed sense of social values. Their inexpensive looking suitcases and "beat up old straw basket" produce a feeling of empathy in him, and lead him to reflect on his own privileged economic status, symbolized by his expensive suitcases. "Everything I had was bourgeois as hell," he muses (15, p. 141).

Holden's relieved that the nuns do not ask him if he's a Catholic. He is able to maintain what Kierkegaard calls his incognito. He tries to have a real conversation with one of the nuns about *Romeo and Juliet* but he's uncomfortable with discussing the "sexy" parts with her. He has trouble reconciling the nun's enjoyment of romantic literature with her sexual abstinence. But instead of retreating into a pseudonymous disguise he stays in the conversation, bridging the aesthetic and the ethical. In the end he resists making up stories about himself and succeeds in having a genuine conversation with her.

Holden admires the ability of the nuns to make commitments in their lives and respects their vows of poverty and chastity: "That's what I liked about those nuns. You could tell for one thing, that they never went anywhere swanky for lunch" (16, p. 149).

In the aesthetic stage, the good life is an attempt to arrange and edit the world so that it can be enjoyed as it is. This may work for a while, but since no one has complete control over the world the aesthetic life inevitably leads to despair. Consequently, the motivation for living the ethical life is to avoid despair.

Those who have made the leap to the ethical realm reconstruct their natures in light of a sense of duty in an act of freedom. According to Kierkegaard, the "leap" to the ethical stage occurs when the moral norms or standards recognized by a given society take priority over the individual's immediate desires for pleasure as the criterion for the good life. The aesthetic way of life is then given up by choosing the ethical life.

When Phoebe asks Holden to choose something he would really like to be, she forces the issue and brings Holden to think about the ethical stage: "'Stop swearing. All right, name something else. Name something you'd like to *be*. Like a scientist. Or a *lawyer* or something,'" she says, (22, p. 223). After some persistence by Phoebe, Holden eventually answers her question:

> "You know what I'd like to be? I mean if I had my goddam choice?"
> "What? Stop *swearing*."
> "You know that song 'If a body catch a body comin' through the rye'? I'd like—"

But when he tells Phoebe that he would like to catch kids in danger of falling over a cliff Holden still remains in the realm of fantasy. He's not yet taking responsibility as an adult and not yet in the ethical realm. He says "if" he had his goddam choice. In order to enter the ethical realm, you must make choices. Holden feels trapped because he does not realize his freedom to make a choice. He has not yet reached the next stage. He's still in transition, in the ironic transition zone.

I Told Him I Was a Real Moron, and All That Stuff

For Kierkegaard, irony finds its voice most effectively with Socrates, who uses irony to undermine the opinions of those who claim to have wisdom and leaves them in a state of bewilderment. He does this by asking questions which ultimately reveal to them their lack of knowledge. Often they become annoyed with him as he induces them to realize they don't have the wisdom they claim to have.

Socrates's use of irony forces them to reflect upon themselves, and to distance themselves from their immediate beliefs and values. Socrates often uses appreciative language when questioning others even if it's clear that they don't know anything. He does this in order not to appear dogmatic and to allow his opponents the opportunity to change their opinions.

Like Socrates, Holden uses ironic language with some of the characters he encounters, and like Socrates he has an idea beforehand that he will not receive the answers that he seeks. The cab driver Horwitz, for example, projects an authoritative demeanor yet knows nothing of what really happens to the ducks or the fish in the lagoon in Central Park in the winter. Holden's questions only irritate Horwitz: "I was afraid he was going to crack the damn taxi up or something. Besides, he was such a touchy guy, it wasn't any pleasure discussing anything with him."

But Holden's opinion of Horwitz takes an ironic turn in the next paragraph. Holden sounds more like Socrates in this ironic statement: "He was a pretty good guy. Quite amusing and all." Ultimately Horwitz is rather short tempered and reactive. "He was about the touchiest guy I ever met. Everything you said made him sore" (12, p. 109). Holden makes the same kind of ambivalent assessment of Maurice, the elevator guy, illustrating the contradictions of irony: "He was a real moron." But a few lines later he says, "He was pretty sharp, in his crumby way. He really was" (14, p. 133–34).

Another aspect of Holden's personality that mirrors Socrates is that he is self-deprecating and never claims to have any knowledge himself. When questioned during his trial, Socrates claims that he knows nothing but that at least he knows that he knows nothing. Holden is quick to admit his flaws and weaknesses, his sexual immaturity and lack of experience. He admits this to old Spencer, his history teacher: "Well, you could see he really felt pretty lousy about flunking me. So I shot the bull for a while. I told him I was a real moron, and all that stuff" (2, p. 17).

Holden's former classmate Carl Luce sounds like one of the Sophists that Socrates encounters. Although Holden describes him as having a good vocabulary he offers nothing but empty, vacuous rhetoric. "Your mind is immature," he tells Holden. "It is. It really is. I know it," Holden replies (19, p. 191). Although he has an attitude of superiority over most of his classmates, and a fondness for referring to others as "morons," Holden often displays a humility about himself and, like Socrates, makes no claims to knowledge.

Socrates claims he has no knowledge but finds flaws in his interlocutor's arguments and pushes them to realize those flaws. His questions are ironic because they seek wisdom but bring out ignorance or negative wisdom. He thus leads them to a greater wisdom, but indirectly. He teaches no theory or doctrine, but rather, like a midwife, helps give birth to what is already inside. Kierkegaard calls Socrates's use of irony "infinite absolute negativity."[4] It is purely negative because he does not give his listeners any new ideals to replace the ones that are rejected. Leaving them with negativity teaches the listeners to develop a new positive world view from within themselves and to be responsible for their own thoughts and values. The early dialogues of Socrates usually reach no positive conclusions and end in deadlock, so it's up to the readers to come up with their own theories to replace what has been refuted. Just as Socrates uses a non-authoritative method of irony to

---

[4] *The Concept of Irony*, p. 271.

avoid establishing himself as a teacher, Kierkegaard uses indirect communication to convey the idea that truth must be apprehended and processed in a subjective, personal way.

I Didn't Follow Her Though I Knew She'd Follow Me

Ironists, according to Kierkegaard, use their narrative talents to prevent a direct relationship between themselves and their listeners. They try to avoid any direct communication of objective knowledge in order to promote an indirect communication that facilitates a passionate inner experience. "Truth is subjectivity," writes Kierkegaard.[5] Truth is only relevant and recognized when it becomes vital to us, the listeners. In a sense, truth is like faith, which bridges the gap between the need for objective certainty and our own subjective passions. And, like faith, it requires a certain capability and receptivity on the part of the listener.

Holden does something similar to this when he leads Phoebe through the streets of New York, allowing her to pretend that she is not following him. He knows that if he tells her directly to follow him she'll refuse. So, thinking like Kierkegaard, he uses an indirect approach: "I didn't follow her though I knew she'd follow *me*, so I started walking downtown toward the zoo, on the park side of the street, and she started walking downtown on the *other* goddam side of the street" (25, p. 270). As a result, Phoebe has the freedom to appropriate the situation as part of her own internal experience, and Holden manages to let her believe that there is no direct communication from him. Allowing Phoebe to walk on the other side of the street enables her to have a subjective experience of something indirectly communicated by Holden.

Holden's strategy reflects Kierkegaard's message that we need to apprehend things subjectively, and be transformed through our own strength of conviction. After Holden reunites with Phoebe he sits on a bench and watches her circling around on a carrousel. He sits in the drenching rain, protected only by his red hunting hat, allowing Phoebe to enjoy the experience of the carrousel on her own terms: "The thing with kids is if they

---

[5] *Concluding Unscientific Postscript,* Volume 2, p. 45.

want to grab for the gold ring, you have to let them do it, and not say anything" (25, pp. 273–74).

As Holden watches the children on the carrousel, he gives up his dream of being a "catcher" and decides to go home and face his parents. Perhaps now he is ready to enter the ethical stage and take responsibility for his life. He has a more mature understanding of the need for children to learn things for themselves. They have to take risks and have personal, passionate experiences in life, and Holden realizes that it is unrealistic and unnatural for him to try to save all children. "If they fall off," he says, "it's bad for you to say anything to them."

Indirect communication, for Kierkegaard, is a strategy for helping others to think deeply about human existence. The listener is forced to appropriate, on a personal level, what is presented, or prompted, by the communicator. Perhaps this is what Salinger accomplishes with this story. We are invited into the inner thoughts of Holden Caulfield, but in order to do so, we have to be receptive to his sarcastic language, adolescent exaggerations and ironic outlook on life. If we accept the invitation and allow ourselves to be initiated, we can be transformed by the narrative. This may partially explain why so many read the book several times throughout their lives. Each time we visit the novel it awakens within us a willingness to take a fresh look at the phoniness that surrounds us and the hypocrisy we encounter in our daily lives.

As readers we must go through what Kierkegaard calls the process of "double reflection" (Volume 1, p. 73). The first stage is to understand things on an intellectual level. The second is to relate this understanding to our own existence. Intellectuals, according to Kierkegaard, have "forgotten what it means to exist, and what inwardness is . . . forgotten what it means to exist humanly" (Volume 1, p. 249). *The Catcher in the Rye* requires us, the readers, to make up our own interpretations of its meanings, to fill the gaps in the story and allow the Holden Caulfields within us to experience the inconsistencies and the underside of life in a way that is tolerable, nostalgic, and beautiful.

For Kierkegaard, receptivity is a process of "emptying the jar" before it can be filled. Intellectuals must first be disabused of the idea that they possess objective truth and convinced to make the objective subjective. Double reflection involves both thinking and existing. In thinking we apprehend universal, objective concepts. But as existing in this thinking we become more inward and subjectively passionate, and appropriate the truth with a willingness to make it part of our existence.

Holden intuits this idea of double reflection with Phoebe: "'C'mon,' I said. 'You feel like dancing?' I taught her how to dance and all when she was a tiny little kid. She's a very good dancer. I mean I just taught her a few things." But the experience of dancing requires a personal passion, and Holden understands that this cannot be taught. "She learned it mostly by herself," he says, ". . . you can't teach somebody how to *really* dance" (23, p. 227).

Holden, through his wit, his sarcasm, and his irony, is able to transcend the immediacy of the aesthetic realm, with its accompanying despair. Watching Phoebe circle on the carrousel he feels "so damn happy." He is able, through the infinite reflective possibilities that irony affords, to make the choices that will hopefully lead him to the ethical realm. Salinger, by presenting us with this narrative, challenges us with the opportunity for double reflection. By "emptying the jar," and emptying our minds of any false hopes about the inauthentic, we too can renew our quest for what is real, genuine, valuable and beautiful.

Holden's
Rules
for
Crumby
Stuff

5
Holden in Love

ELIZABETH OLSON and CHARLES TALIAFERRO

One of the most frustrating—and entertaining—aspects of Holden Caulfield's odyssey in *Catcher in the Rye* is watching him try on vices that seem to him to represent being grown up.

Phoniness, reckless or illicit sex, profligate spending—all vices of the adult world—appear irresistible to Holden, even as he loudly and definitively disdains them. And they all go badly for the young man as he tries on these different aspects of adulthood. Compounding the problem, Holden seems to lack all self-awareness of the love-hate relationship he has with those traits that he in many ways perceives to be synonymous with adulthood.

But Holden also highlights the vices of childhood—irrationality, cruelty, and selfishness—as he hurtles toward that most undesirable outcome, adulthood. To what extent are there virtues and vices that are very specific to children as opposed to grown-ups? In the end, as the book's argument implies, perhaps only a powerful love can overcome the vices of both childhood and adulthood.

Catcher in the Rye is an ideal book for addressing virtues and vices and the transition from childhood to adulthood because of Holden's pronounced character flaws and because of his ambivalence about being a boy fast-approaching adulthood. He is, throughout the book, unable to hang on to the virtues and vices of childhood, and deeply conflicted about the very adult process of negotiating the line between virtue and vice.

The book also has a surprising mix of humor and seriousness, which gives *Catcher* buoyancy and suspense. You can pic-

ture a movie based on the book done to very comic effect, except
for the poignant addition of Holden's sad family, brokenhearted
by the tragic death of the son Allie. Also, there's a sense of tension caused by the fear that Holden might not make it—he may
well become the horribly bitter man his former English teacher
warns against, and this dampens the potentially comic under-
tone of a young man on a tear in New York City, trying to hire
a prostitute, trying to impress stupid young women, trying to
dance and drink until he jollies himself into a good time.

Life on the Border between Childhood and Adulthood

Early in the book, the mention of the novel *Out of Africa*, by
Isak Dinesen, is telling. The novel is about love, marriage,
betrayal, a failed business, romance, and death. It offers a wist-
ful, almost mournful portrait of an exotic time and place, with
themes of loss of innocence and the failure of worldly ambition,
not boyhood adventure or optimistic romance. But in later discussion about her life in Africa, Dinesen also famously articulated some of Holden's yearnings:

> Here at long last one was in a position not to give a damn for all con-
> ventions, here was a new kind of freedom which until then one had
> only found in dreams! (Quoted in Donald Hannah, *Isak Dinesen and
> Karen Blixen*, Random House, 1971, p. 207)

The reference to *Out of Africa* in *Catcher in the Rye* provides a
useful first glimpse into Holden's awkward perch between
phases of his life, his desire for freedom from convention in a
way that demands no sacrifice.

At sixteen years old, Holden is a teenager who poses as a
person who is at least eighteen. Holden wants to act older than
he is, but he also loathes aging when this involves decline—he
seems disgusted by his teacher's weak condition at the beginning of the book.

> . . . there were pills and medicine all over the place, and everything
> smelled like Vicks Nose Drops. . . . What made it even more depress-
> ing, old Spencer had on this very sad, ratty old bathrobe that he was
> probably born in or something. I don't much like to see old guys in

their pajamas and bathrobes anyway. Their bumpy old chests are always showing. (2, p. 11)

And yet, Holden himself is not the picture of youthful health and vigor. Physically speaking, Holden smokes so much that it impedes his running. He has gray hair—something that helps him pass for someone of drinking age. Holden tries to look like an adult, but he has the teenager's preoccupation with awkward bodily processes (such as pimples and cutting his nails). And despite some success *looking* older than his years, Holden does not possess many of the advantages of actual maturity. He seems unable to handle alcohol (he gets quite drunk in Chapter 20), and he is inept at something as simple as taking a taxi ride (the relationship between driver and Holden as passenger breaks down twice, in Chapters 9 and 12). His anger ranges from mere irritation to outright rage, but when it spills over into physical combat he fights more like a child than a man and is easily overcome (first by Stradlater, then by Maurice).

Holden's attitude to religion has a kind of adolescent ambivalence compared with either a simple childhood faith (or lack of faith) or a mature adult commitment to faith (or lack of faith). For example, while he is quite negative about institutional religion, he also wonders whether one might join a monastery without being Roman Catholic (side note: yes, you can; there are Anglican and Orthodox monasteries) at a point in the story when you get the feeling he might just like to try on the monastic life (though perhaps the moment only lasts for a few minutes). At one point he feels like praying (Chapter 14), and he is impressed by and gives money to some nuns.

Holden is a virgin who has a glimpse of how sex or at least sensuality can be innocent and fulfilling, even redemptive, in the recollection of holding Jane's hand and kissing her after Jane's alcoholic stepfather interrupts their checkers game. But despite this brief look at what might be an authentically fulfilling, life-enhancing partnership, Holden's experiences with sex are quite disastrous. At the hotel he observes sexual acts that seem demeaning (a man and a woman spitting drinks at each other's faces) or confusing (cross-dressing). In his own case, the sexual acts designed to arouse him are performed unsuccessfully by a prostitute.

In ways physical, behavioral, spiritual, and experiential, Holden sits most uneasily on the threshold of adulthood. He lacks adult competence—in social intercourse, work, and sex—but he has some adult desires and goals and is not comfortable being thought of as a child. Holden is not, in fact, comfortable with much of anything.

Integrity, Phoniness, and Love

In addition to sitting—very awkwardly—on the cusp of adulthood, Holden badly wants to connect with someone in a genuine way, without pretense and without phoniness, but he simply cannot. He fondly remembers the connections he had with his brother Allie, with Jane, and with his young sister Phoebe. But now, and at all the schools he has been at, he cannot make connections in any real way, and it is as though he projects his own inability to connect and be genuine onto other people, who are all phonies. Even as he calls the rest of the world (peers and older adults, never young kids or family) phonies, he boasts about how good he is at lying.

> I'm the most terrific liar you ever saw in your life. . . . If I'm on my way to the store . . . and somebody asks me where I'm going, I'm liable to say I'm going to the opera. . . . So when I told old Spencer I had to go to the gym to get my equipment and stuff, that was a sheer lie. I don't even keep my goddam equipment in the gym. (3, p. 22)

Holden's conversation with Eddie Morrow's mother on the train after he leaves Pencey Prep, when he takes on a whole different persona, is only the first of many instances in the book in which he is not truthful about what he wants, what he's doing, or who he is (he tells her his name is Rudolf Schmidt, the name of the school janitor). This is no doubt because Holden doesn't know what he wants, what he's doing, or who he is.

The train conversation is the first of several instances to raise the question of how believable Holden's dislike of phoniness really is. He perhaps senses the flip side of the vice of phoniness, which is the virtue of civility or integrity. For instance, although Holden roundly criticizes Sally as a phony while she is on a date with him and she notices and talks to another young man, there is no evidence that she's doing anything other than being polite to an old acquaintance. Holden assumes phoniness in what may simply be what the administration at a prep school might describe as good breeding. Adults walk this tightrope all the time, and far from indicating they've sold out or are phonies, it may simply be one way to make the world a little more pleasant and workable.

One key to understanding Holden's ambivalence about phoniness lies in the role of love in childhood and adulthood. As a child, love may be present or absent in response to the good of others, and it enjoys (at its best) a kind of innocence. This is perhaps brought out with Holden's vision of the Catcher in the Rye. He thinks there is a great good in children playing freely and also in adults or at least someone (the Catcher) rescuing them when they're in trouble.

For children, love of others is necessarily more limited than for adults in the sense that, for example, a child cannot love a person for their twenty years of faithful companionship nor do they usually love unilaterally. A child's love may be no less powerful than an adult's—and may be purer and more unconditional—but it rarely occurs with an adult's understanding of flaws, joy, or reconciliation—the *context* in which adults love.

Holden takes an optimistic if small step toward the virtues of adulthood when, in his encounter with Phoebe near the end of the book, he begins to think of others in relation to himself with some detachment and the beginnings of generosity.

> I started giving her the rest of the dough she'd lent me. "You keep it. Keep it for me," she said. Then she said right afterward—"Please." That's depressing, when somebody says "please" to you. I mean if it's Phoebe or somebody. That depressed the hell out of me. But I put the dough back in my pocket. (25, p. 272)

In Phoebe ("old Phoebe" as Holden refers to her) Holden sees a genuine, if unacknowledged, version of mature love. And once adult love—encompassing generosity and human failings and joy in companionship—is in the picture, we as readers see a way for Holden to achieve genuine connection and live with integrity and the rites of forgiveness and reconciliation.

Prior to his interaction with Phoebe, Holden seems quite ambivalent about love—the word occurs rarely in the book, sometimes only in passing (Chapter 10). But he eventually begins to understand the challenge of integrity as a child and as an adult, and in the relationship with Phoebe it is hard not to see his happiness (in the penultimate chapter) in terms of an authentic love.

The Virtues and Vices of Money

Holden's relationship with money is another fascinating study in contradictions. He clearly comes from wealth, but does not want (or need) to acknowledge the value of money, and he seems to do his best to get rid of any money he has. He spends profligately on hotels, bars, shows, bars, cabs, and bars.

Holden is not naïve, though. His disdain for money is in stark contrast to his description of an old roommate's cheap luggage—which conveys a razor sharp understanding of class and what money really buys a person:

> . . . when I was at Elkton Hills, I roomed with this boy, Dick Slagle, that had these very inexpensive suitcases. He used to keep them under the bed, instead of on the rack, so that nobody'd see them standing next to mine. It depressed the holy hell out of me. . . . The thing is, it's really hard to be roommates with people if your suitcases are much better than theirs. . . . You think if they're intelligent and all, the other person, and have a good sense of humor, that they don't give a damn whose suitcases are better, but they do. They really do. (15, pp. 141–42)

His only positive or "pure" interactions with people in the book are those with people who either don't have or don't value money—his sister Phoebe for example, or the nuns he meets at the diner. Holden obviously admires the nuns (both of whom lack position, prestige, or sex appeal), and he explicitly admires their selflessness and wonders at their lack of money. Interestingly, money changes hands, but with a great deal of ambivalence and awkwardness on Holden's part:

> "I thought if you were taking up a collection," I told her, "I could make a small contribution . . ." . . . They let me give them ten bucks as a contribution. They kept asking me if I was sure I could afford it. . . . They took it, though, finally. The both of them kept thanking me so much it was embarrassing. . . . I took their check off them, but they wouldn't let me pay it. . . . After they left, I started getting sorry that I'd only given them ten bucks for their collection. But the thing was, I'd made

that date to go to a matinee with old Sally Hayes, and I needed to
keep some dough for the tickets and stuff. . . . Goddam money. It
always ends up making you blue as hell. (15, pp. 143–47)

When Phoebe gives Holden her Christmas money, it is as
though for the first time Holden understands that money
might mean something to someone without it corrupting that
person. He's determined to repay Phoebe, implying that he
knows the money might be important or useful to her, but he
does not fault her for this. He takes on a small amount of
responsibility for repaying her, in another small step toward
maturity, perhaps.

If we can see a very limited relationship with money as a
virtue of childhood (that is, no corruption of filthy lucre), it may
be easy to assume greed as the correlating adult vice. But in
Holden's case, his adult vice is not greed, but almost a denial of
the value of money—profligate, silly spending when he clearly
sees and experiences the benefits of wealth. All the while, he
disdains the work, motive, and sacrifices and/or luck necessary
to have accumulated that wealth off of which he lives. You
can't—and shouldn't—have it both ways—excessive spending
and disdain for wealth—for long.

Holden seems to be beginning to understand that money is
a complex thing, capable of inciting all manner of bad behavior:
dull living, greed, corruption, phoniness (there's that word
again . . .), but he doesn't make the connection in a meaningful
way to the idea that there may be some value in earning a living, in controlling your money and making choices about it.
Holden's periodic fantasies about running away and living in
the woods indicate the beginnings of his desire to control this
aspect of his life. This, combined with the generosity that is
part and parcel of his profligate spending, indicates Holden has
some of the necessary puzzle pieces available with which to
approach the adult virtue of controlling his economic destiny in
a larger sense, not just succumbing to greed or letting the love
of money control his life.

Vice versus Virtue

Childhood and adulthood come with their own vexing liabilities
and opportunities, but in its treatment of each, *Catcher in the*

Rye points to (and this may be no more than a hint) the anti-dote of self-controlled, loving generosity. The apex of Holden's journey to this loving generosity seems to crystallize (in Chapter 25) when Holden finds happiness enjoying Phoebe play on the carrousel, even if Chapter 26 doesn't offer a full guarantee of Holden's maturation.

In the eighteenth century Edmund Burke famously wrote that wickedness is a vice that can be manifested at different times in different fashions, which connects to *Catcher*'s point about self-controlled loving generosity.

> Seldom have two ages the same fashion in their pretexts and the same modes of mischief. Wickedness is a little more inventive. Whilst you are discussing fashion, the fashion is gone by. The very same vice assumes a new body. The spirit transmigrates; and, far from los-ing its principle of life by the change of its appearance, it is renovated in its new organs with the fresh vigour of a juvenile activity. It walks abroad; it continues its ravages; whilst you are gibbeting the carcass, or demolishing the tomb. You are terrifying yourself with ghosts and apparitions, whilst your house is the haunt of robbers. It is thus with all those, who, attending only to the shell and husk of history, think they are waging war with intolerance, pride, and cruelty, whilst, under colour of abhorring the ill principles of antiquated parties, they are authorizing and feeding the same odious vices in different factions, and perhaps in worse. (*Reflections on the Revolution in France*, Hackett, 1987, pp. 124–25)

Maybe Burke's right and there's a common link between the vices that are in fashion at different times and places; perhaps wickedness dwells deep down under different disguises. But whether he's right or wrong, as children or adults a self-con-trolled loving generosity should be the powerful virtue of choice.

Paraphrasing Burke: seldom are the fashions of childhood and adulthood the same and yet, come what may, self-con-trolled loving generosity is an inventive powerful virtue that can involve important manifestations at all times, whether or not you have just gotten kicked out of a prep school and are on your way to New York City.[1]

---

[1] We're grateful to Olivia James for her editorial assistance.

6
Holden and Some Very Crumby Stuff

KEITH DROMM

In Chapter 9 of *The Catcher in the Rye,* Holden admits to us that he's "probably the biggest sex maniac" we've ever seen (9, p. 81).

This revelation is prompted by the "crumby" acts he sees out his window taking place in the other rooms at the Edmont Hotel. An older man is walking around his room in high heels and women's clothes. In another room, a man and woman are squirting water or highballs through their mouths into each other's faces. Holden tells us that he can also "think of *very* crumby stuff" he "wouldn't mind doing if the opportunity came up." Even squirting water in a women's face might be "quite a lot of fun," but he tells us: "The thing is, though, I don't *like* the idea" (9, p. 81). By saying he doesn't like the idea, even though it would be a lot of fun, Holden seems to be expressing a *moral* objection to squirting water in a sex partner's face. He has objections to other crumby stuff; he later tells us that he has all sorts of "sex rules" (9, p. 82) and "principles" (13, p. 119), even though he doesn't follow them all the time.

These "sex rules" make up Holden's *sexual ethics.* It's a characteristic of such rules that they don't always conform to what we want to do, even those things we think would be a lot of fun. They are rules about what we *should* do. We follow them in order to be moral. We might think that acting morally will ultimately be "fun" or in some other ways make us happy. Or we might think that there are other reasons for being moral, such as obligations we have to others, ourselves, or a god.

One implication of such moral rules is that we believe they hold for everyone. Everyone reading this chapter likely believes that killing an innocent person is wrong, but we don't just believe that it's wrong for each of us, individually, to murder. We believe it is wrong for *anyone* to murder. That's why we punish people who murder and in other ways try to dissuade or prevent them from murdering. In contrast, some of us might believe that scotch and sodas don't taste very good. We don't drink them, but we don't think there's anything wrong with Holden or others drinking them. We might not understand why they drink them, but we don't typically criticize them or try to punish them for drinking them (unless they drink too much of them); it's merely a matter of people's different tastes. We *do* enforce our beliefs about what's moral in one or both of these ways.

Holden appears to believe that his "sex rules" apply to everyone else, or in other words, that they are *universal*. One piece of evidence for this is his reaction to Stradlater "giving the time" to Jane Gallagher. He throws a punch at him and calls him a "dirty stupid sonuvabitch of a moron" (6, p. 58). Holden's reaction to Stradlater's behavior towards Jean suggests that he believes it's *morally* wrong. He tries to punish Stradlater for it (but he just ends up getting himself a bloody nose from Stradlater). The best explanation for Holden's reaction is that he believes it is wrong for Stradlater or anyone else to treat a person this way; that it is something much worse than drinking Tom Collinses in the middle of December.[1]

We can evaluate Holden's "sex rules" and not merely identify them. That is, we can ask whether these are the right rules to have. In doing so, we're concerned not only with whether Holden should follow these rules, but whether we should as well. So, after identifying and evaluating Holden's rules, we should become more familiar with both Holden's and our own sexual ethics.

Stopping when Someone Says "Stop"

Holden tell us that "The trouble with me is, I stop" (13, p. 120) whenever a girl tells him to stop. The "trouble" this has caused

---

[1] As did two of the girls he danced with in the Lavender Room, but Holden tells us: "They didn't know any better" (10, p. 97).

for Holden—as he finally reveals in Chapter 13—is that it's
kept him a virgin. But, while it might be the reason for his virginity, it's a good thing that he stops when the other says to
stop. This shows him to be someone who respects the *consent* of
his sexual partners: "Most guys don't. I can't help it" (13, p.
120). A core principle in sexual ethics is that the sexual behaviors we engage in with others are only morally permissible
when all the parties consent to them. We shouldn't do crumby
stuff to another person unless he or she wants us to.

Determining whether there is consent is sometimes difficult. As Holden explains, "You never know whether they really
want you to stop, or whether they're just scared as hell, or
whether they're just telling you to stop so that if you *do* go
through with it, the blame'll be on *you*, not them" (13, pp.
120–21). Holden, however, goes by the good rule that if someone says "stop" (or "no," or any variation on these), you should
understand it to *mean* stop; so not yes, or maybe, or if you just
persist I might eventually say "yes." Lack of consent can also be
expressed non-verbally. Physical resistance or just passivity
can mean "stop." A "don't stop" or a "yes" or a "let's go" (as
Sunny the prostitute says to Holden, p. 124) can express consent, but an explicit verbal expression of consent isn't necessary; there are many non-verbal ways of expressing consent. If
it isn't clear whether someone's consenting, then the other person is obligated to stop what he or she is doing and ask the person directly whether it's okay to continue. If he doesn't receive
a clear expression of consent, he should stop.

A person's lack of consent to having some action performed
on him doesn't always prohibit us from performing it. For
example, a criminal about to be arrested might not consent to
being thrown in jail, but we don't need his consent to do so. But
there's never a case where a person's refusal to have a sexual
act performed upon them does not make that act impermissible. There was a time when marital rape, a husband forcing his
wife to have sex, was not considered by many to be either
immoral or illegal, but we now believe that a person can refuse
to consent to sex with a spouse. Sex is such an intimate activity and one with such serious potential consequences (for
example, pregnancy) that the unwillingness of the parties to
engage in it can never be ignored.

Holden's appreciation of the seriousness of sex is perhaps reflected in his efforts to erase the "Fuck you"s written on the wall at Phoebe's school:

It drove me damn near crazy. I thought how Phoebe and all the other little kids would see it, and how they'd wonder what the hell it meant, and then finally some dirty kid would tell them—all cockeyed, naturally—what it meant, and how they'd all *think* about it and maybe even *worry* about it for a couple of days. (25, pp. 260–61)

He even imagines catching the guy who did it and smashing his head on the stone steps "till he was good and goddam dead and bloody" (25, p. 261). Like his reaction to Stradlater's "giving the time" to Jane Gallagher, this suggests that he has a moral objection to writing "Fuck you" and other sexually explicit messages where children can see it. More generally, he seems to believe that we have a moral obligation to protect children from the knowledge of sex. His own experiences have taught him the emotional pains and other difficulties it entails.

In addition to sex, there are various other actions that we cannot perform on others without their consent, such as medical experimentation. We cannot test experimental drugs on a person, for example, unless she gives consent. This and other types of medical experiment are similar to sex in using the body in intimate ways with potentially serious, long-term consequences. In order for a person to consent to have her body used in these ways, she must be aware of all the possible consequences. Any *expression* of consent by the person without this information is not consent. We see in a later section of this chapter how incomplete or false information can invalidate expressions of consent in sexual encounters.

Getting in Some Practice

In Chapter 13, Holden accepts the elevator guy's offer of five bucks for a "throw" with a prostitute (13, p. 119). Holden figures that since he's a virgin, by having sex with the prostitute he "could get in some practice on her, in case I ever get married or anything" (13, p. 121). He recalls this book he read once about a Monsieur Blanchard, who lives in a chateau on the

Riviera and spends most of his spare time having sex with women. Blanchard is well beyond needing any practice with women; Holden tells us how Blanchard compares his ability to that of a gifted violinist and a woman's body to a violin. Even though Holden admits that this sounds corny, "it isn't *too* corny" and he "wouldn't mind being pretty good at that stuff" (13, p. 121). But when the prostitute, Sunny, shows up, he's unable to go through with it.

Various things might have caused Holden to change his mind about having sex with a prostitute. In his *Confessions*, the philosopher Jean-Jacques Rousseau (1712–1778) can be just as revealing as Holden, and he tells us: "A women who could be bought for money would lose all her charm for me; I doubt if I even have it in me to take advantage of her."[2] Holden might also find it distasteful to have sex with a prostitute, and when Sunny "started getting funny. . . . Crude and all" (13, p. 126), his not getting aroused might have revealed this to him. In sharing his views about prostitutes, Rousseau is describing his "particular taste for things" and explaining why he takes no pleasure in things that can be bought: "money poisons everything." While Holden might share Rousseau's tastes, he also tells us that having sex with a prostitute is "against his principles" (13, p. 119). As I pointed out earlier, there is a difference between tastes and principles.

One source of moral principles is religion and many religions proscribe sex outside of marriage, whether it's with a prostitute or for free. Many people get their moral beliefs—or at least a core set of them—through their religions, typically the commands of their god or gods as recorded in scripture or revelation. However, religious beliefs do not seem to be the source of Holden's "principles." He tells us that he's "sort of an atheist" (14, p. 130). He says this right after Sunny leaves and he tries—but fails—to pray. He then explains how he likes Jesus but the Disciples in the Bible "annoy the hell" out of him.

There must be some non-religious basis to his principle against prostitution, like some more general moral principle. Uncertainty about Sunny's consent might be the reason why he decides not to have sex with her. We know that he has a

---

[2] *Confessions*, Oxford University Press, 2000, p. 35.

principle against having sex with persons without their consent. However, she walks into his room under her own power. She seems willing to have sex with him and even appears impatient with Holden (or "Jim Steele," as he identifies himself to her) when he doesn't follow through, twice giving what appears to be a verbal expression of consent, although not a very enthusiastic one: "Let's go, hey" (13, pp. 124, 125).

But even such apparent expressions of consent cannot always be guarantees of actual consent. We consider certain groups of people incapable of consenting to sexual activity. These are people who do not have the cognitive ability to understand the consequences of certain actions or even the actions themselves. Children are among such people, as well as the mentally impaired. Among the latter, we include not only those who have a mental disability, but also those suffering from a temporary mental impairment, such as someone who's intoxicated. Even a "don't stop," a "yes," or a "let's go, hey" from such persons does not constitute consent.

Now, Sunny doesn't appear to be drunk; she also seems mentally competent. However, according to Holden, "she was young as hell" (13, p. 123). He thinks she's his age, which is sixteen. Legally and probably otherwise, this is too young to consent to sexual activity. Her age is not the only thing that might invalidate her apparent expressions of consent. Prostitution is not always a choice; various things can coerce someone into prostitution. We don't understand her relationship with Maurice; so, for example, we don't know what he might have said to her to get her to go to Holden's hotel room late at night. He could have threatened her somehow. This would invalidate her expressions of apparent consent. We also don't know what other factors might have influenced her into becoming a prostitute; drug addiction or economic conditions can force someone into prostitution.

Even if these circumstances are not coercive—that is, they do not make their victim incapable of consenting to the actions they influence—having sex with a prostitute might count as *exploitation*. Rousseau expresses this idea when he writes, "I doubt if I even have it in me to take advantage of her." To take advantage of someone is to exploit her vulnerable situation in order to benefit yourself, rather than helping them out of that situation.

However, Holden doesn't give expression to any of these reasons for not having sex with Sunny. He only tells us, after concluding the deal with Maurice, that "It was against my principles and all, but I was feeling so depressed I didn't even *think*" (13, p. 119). But he doesn't tell us what specific principle he failed to think about when he hired the prostitute. It could be the case that Holden is wrong; despite what he says, he has no moral objection to prostitution. It often happens that someone claims to have a moral objection to something, but when pressed for the reasons behind it, they are unable to state what these are. The person is then compelled to conclude that they don't really hold such a moral principle and were wrong to think that they did. Still, something prevented Holden from "getting in some practice" with Sunny. It might be a moral principle that has nothing to do with prostitution.

Necking with Phonies

In attempting to explain why he didn't have sex with Sunny, Holden tells us:

> The trouble was, I just didn't want to do it. I felt more depressed than sexy, if you want to know the truth. *She* was depressing. Her green dress hanging in the closet and all. And besides, I don't think I could *ever* do it with somebody that sits in a stupid movie all day long. I really don't think I could. (13, p. 125)

Holden doesn't like Sunny. Besides being depressing, she likes the movies. We know that Holden is no fan of the movies: "If there's one thing I hate, it's the movies" (1, p. 4). He also calls her "a pretty spooky kid" (13, p. 127). Later in the novel, Holden tells Luce, his former student advisor at Whooton, "I can never get really sexy—I mean *really* sexy—with a girl I don't like a lot"; if he doesn't like her, he loses his "goddam desire for her and all" (19, p. 191). So, in the same way that Rousseau's paying for something causes him to lose interest in it, Holden's not liking a girl causes him to lose his sexual interest in her. But Holden might also be inhibited from having sex with Sunny by a moral principle that he explains elsewhere.

After watching the couple squirt water in each other's faces, Holden tells us:

I think if you don't really like a girl, you shouldn't horse around with
her at all, and if you *do* like her, then you're supposed to like her face,
and if you like her face, you ought to be careful about doing crumby
stuff to it, like squirting water all over it. (9, p. 81)

He then shares with us one of his "sex rules": "Last year I made
a rule that I was going to quit horsing around with girls that,
deep down, gave me a pain in the ass" (9, p. 82). He broke the
rule the same day he made it. Nevertheless, given what he says
about the couple in the other room, he still thinks it's wrong to
engage in sexual activity with a person you don't like. So, he
not only lost his "goddam desire" for Sunny, having sex with her
would violate this sex rule.[3]

But what's wrong with having sex with a person you don't
like? Holden tells us he broke the rule when he "spent the
whole night necking with a terrible phony named Anne Louise
Sherman" (9, p. 82). Holden, we all know, doesn't like phonies.
Necking with them might make him a sort of hypocrite. It can
also encourage them. But necking with phonies does these
things because it implicitly expresses approval of them. That's
its real problem.

If someone has sex with you because you've let them
wrongly believe that you like them, then their consent isn't
genuine. Perhaps Anne Louise Sherman wouldn't have
necked with Holden if she knew he thought she was a phony.
If he let her believe that he did like her, he deceived her.
Expressions of consent that are a result of deception are not
genuine. Recall the comparison with medical experimentation that we made earlier. If someone agrees to be a subject
in a medical experiment but they are not fully informed
about the nature of the experiment, especially its consequences, then they haven't actually consented. The subject is
like the mentally deficient person who can't consent because
they don't fully understand what they're consenting to. In
the case of the medical experiment, the subject's mental defi-
ciency, so to speak, is caused by the experimenters; they
haven't given the subject complete information about the
experiment. This is why there are many moral and legal

---

[3] Another explanation for why Holden couldn't have sex with Sunny is
given in Chapter 7 of this volume.

guidelines about obtaining consents from subjects in medical and other sorts of experiments.

Sexual partners should also be fully informed. There are various things sexual partners can deceive each other about, for example, STDs, their marital status, and so on. Holden's "sex rule" says you shouldn't deceive another person about your feelings about him or her. If you don't like the other person, you should let them know. You shouldn't withhold this information because it often figures in other people's decisions about whether to have sex. Many people don't want to have sex with someone who doesn't like them.

This could be a reason for Holden's anger at Stradlater for "giving the time" to Jane Gallagher. His anger could be an expression of his jealousy, but it could also be due to what he sees as "unscrupulous" Stradlater's violation of this principle (6, p. 52). When they're fighting, Holden screams at him: "You don't even know if her first name is Jane or *Jean*, ya goddam moron!" (6, p. 57). He also told him that "he didn't care if a girl kept all her kings in the back row or not," an important aspect of her personality according to Holden. Stradlater's ignorance about Jane reveals his lack of positive feelings for her; he doesn't really like her. Holden perhaps suspects that Stradlater has given Jane the opposite impression in order to get "sexy" with her.

However, what if the other person doesn't like you, and she doesn't care whether you like her? Perhaps Anne Louise Sherman knew that Holden thought she was a phony, but she just wanted to neck and it made no difference to her what Holden thought of her. If that's the case, then Holden hasn't deceived her about his feelings; there's no problem with Anne Louise Sherman's consent. But Holden seems to think that regardless of their consent, you should still respect the people you have sex with. When he's talking with Luce, he criticizes him for calling an ex-girlfriend a whore: "'If she was decent enough to let you get sexy with her all the time, you at least shouldn't talk about her that way'" (19, p. 188). When he comments on the couple squirting water in each other's faces, he says "if you *do* like her, then you're supposed to like her face, and if you like her face, you ought to be careful about doing crumby stuff to it, like squirting water all over it" (9, p. 81). These remarks suggest a moral principle that goes beyond the one about consent. He seems to be saying that sexual partners should like each other. What could be the basis of this principle?

I think that Holden is expressing a sexist attitude about sex. He seems to think that women, in having sex with men, are doing them some sort of favor. At the basis of this attitude is the male-chauvinist view that women don't have their own sexual desires. Maybe that woman likes to have water squirted in her face. While it's not nice to call someone a whore, maybe Luce's ex-girlfriend wasn't "being decent enough" to have sex with Luce; she *wanted* to have sex with him. Of course you should respect the people you have sex with, but you should respect everyone. Just because a woman has sex with a man doesn't mean he owes her some extra respect. His having sex with her and "being pretty good" (13, p. 121) at it is enough gratitude.

"Flits" and "Perverts"

Holden not only seems sexist at times, he can also be homophobic. In several places in the novel, Holden uses the derogatory term "flits" to refer to homosexuals. For example, when he is at the Wicker Bar waiting for Luce to show up, he notices that the "other end of the bar was full of flits" (19, p. 185). Luce used to incite Holden's homophobia with the "sex talks" that he delivered late at night at Whooton; they typically included Luce telling them about everyone that was either gay or lesbian in the world:

> He said half the married guys in the world were flits and didn't even know it. He said you could turn into one practically overnight, if you had all the traits and all. He used to scare the hell out of us. I kept waiting to turn into a flit or something. (19, p. 186)

Holden has a fear of gays (which I suspect in most cases is, as Holden's remarks suggest, really a fear of *becoming* gay), but he never articulates a moral objection to homosexuality. People who have a fear of homosexuality often mistake that fear for a moral objection. We often do the same with "perverts," which Holden seems to use as a broader category for homosexuals and others. We can't infer a moral objection to homosexuality from any of the moral principles he does articulate. It doesn't violate his consent principle, his supposed principle against sex with prostitutes, or his principle about liking the person you have sex with; it's also not analogous to writing "Fuck You" on the walls of a children's school.

However, at one point in the novel he responds to the actions of an apparent homosexual as if they were a violation of some moral principle. This is when Mr. Antolini appears to make a pass at him. Holden wakes up on Mr. Antolini's couch to find him stroking his hair. Holden's reaction to this is different than a typical one to an unwelcomed sexual advance. These sometimes surprise us, and they usually make us uncomfortable and embarrassed. Holden feels these ways; for example, he says, "It was very embarrassing" (24, p. 251). But his reaction is even stronger:

> Boy, I was shaking like a madman. I was sweating, too. When something perverty like that happens, I start sweating like a bastard. That kind of stuff's happened to me about twenty times since I was a kid. I can't stand it. (24, p. 251)

There are various things besides a moral objection that could explain Holden's reaction to Mr. Antolini's apparent sexual advance, but his belief that Mr. Antolini has done something *wrong* is one explanation. Mr. Antolini doesn't think he's done anything wrong. He doesn't offer an apology. Instead, he keeps repeating that Holden is a "very, very strange boy" (24, pp. 250-51). Could there by anything wrong with Mr. Antolini's actions?[4]

Holden went to Mr. Antolini seeking advice and encouragement. He gets these things, and in giving them Mr. Antolini is fulfilling his obligations as Holden's teacher. Even though Holden left Elkton Hills a while ago, Mr. Antolini still serves the same role in Holden's life and he's aware of that. When Holden shows up at the Antolinis', it's clear that he is in need and he's not just there to socialize or have sex. Mr. Antolini identifies this need when he tells Holden, "I have a

---

[4] I'm assuming that Antolini was making a pass at Holden. Maybe he wasn't, but that's how Holden perceived it (although he has second thoughts about this after he leaves, 25, p. 253) and I'm looking at the way he thinks in order to discover more about his sexual ethics.

feeling that you're riding for some kind of a terrible, terrible fall" (24: 242). He gives Holden some advice for avoiding this fall.

Among a teacher's obligations is to give accurate and helpful advice and encouragement to his or her students. This is probably the most important and defining obligation of a teacher. However, when that advice and encouragement is combined with a sexual advance, it tends to confuse it. The student can reasonably question its sincerity. Sexual seduction is often insincere. It consists of flattery, which might be truthful, but its source—the seducer—is not reliable. He might not be trying to deceive—as Stradlater does Jane—but his sexual desire makes his evaluations of the other less objective. The target of those desires can understand this and not regard those evaluations as reliable. In making a pass at Holden, Mr. Antolini has made himself an unreliable advisor to Holden. He has thrown into doubt all of that information that might save him from that "terrible fall." His attempt to seduce Holden (if that's what it was) has corrupted, so to speak, this advice. Mr. Antolini has failed in his obligation to give accurate and helpful advice to a student.

Mr. Antolini actions are not wrong because they are directed against another male; they are wrong because they are directed against a student. It's not only that this student is under-age that makes them wrong. Even if Holden were older, Mr. Antolini's actions would undermine the obligations he has towards Holden as his teacher. It's not clear whether Holden recognizes any of this. His reaction to Mr. Antolini's actions might just be an expression of his homophobia. But Holden might see them as a violation of the principle we are articulating; at least, this principle is not inconsistent with any of his more clearly stated principles.

Are Holden's Sex Rules the Right Ones?

We've identified a set of principles that make up Holden's sexual ethics. There are likely many more principles that comprise his sexual ethics, but these are the ones he gives expression to, either implicitly or explicitly, in the novel. To summarize:

1. Stop when the other says stop

2. Don't tell children about sex

3. Don't have sex with prostitutes

4. Don't have sex with people you don't like

5. Be nice to the people you have sex with

6. Don't be a "flit"

7. Don't be a Mr. Antolini

Not all of these are good rules. Some of them Holden probably doesn't really hold. It seems that he doesn't really have moral objections to prostitution or homosexuality. There are two versions of #4. We concluded that the best version is the one that holds that we shouldn't deceive others about our feelings for them in order to get them to consent to sex with us.

Holden also seems to believe that even when you haven't deceived the other person about your feelings, you should only have sex with her if you like her. We couldn't find any good reasons for this version of the rule. #5 is connected to it. It's a good rule, but one you should apply to everybody, not just those you have sex with. If Holden believes that women deserve some extra consideration for having sex with you, then he's probably being sexist.

#1 and #2 are the ones he most clearly holds. With various qualifications, #2 is a good rule. Any sort of information that they can't make use of, and which will only distress them, should be withheld from children. #1 is the best and most important of the rules, because it underlies many of the other rules that comprise sexual ethics. For example, it's the basis of #4.

As in many other areas of his life, Holden isn't fully mature when it comes to moral reasoning. However, he has what's essential for being moral, an awareness of and concern for other people's feelings. The former is evident, for example, in his conversation with Ernest Morrow's mother on the train to New York. Even though he tells mostly lies about her son and doesn't share with her his view that her son is "doubtless the biggest bastard that ever went to Pency" (8, p. 71), he does these things because he's aware of this about all mothers' feelings for their sons: "all they want to hear about is what a hot-shot their son is" (8, p. 73).

Holden's lies reveal his concern for other people's feelings, as do his sex rules. So, while he might falter in articulating and identifying his sex and other moral rules, he at least tries to act in ways that take other people's feelings into account. This is the primary purpose of morality, to prescribe modifications to our behavior that will accommodate the feelings and other interests of those with whom we interact. In his attacks on "phonies" and various others, Holden reveals a greater appreciation of the importance of this than many of the other people, especially the adults, in his world.

7
The Moral Call and the Moral Catch

GUY PINKU

If you really love the *Catcher in the Rye*, you may not feel like analyzing it too much. As Holden says, when describing the feeling of being different each time he visits the museum: "I mean you'd be *diff*erent in some way—I can't explain what I mean. And even if I could, I'm not sure I'd feel like it" (16, p. 158).

Yet Holden's observations and actions do display a philosophical point of view. Holden has a moral attitude close to the one developed in *Totality and Infinity*,[1] a book which the philosopher Emanuel Levinas published in 1961, ten years after *The Catcher*.

Both J.D. Salinger and Emanuel Levinas witnessed the moral collapse of humanity during the Second World War (Levinas was kept as a prisoner; Salinger served in the US army and was among the first soldiers to enter a liberated concentration camp). We can see traces of these experiences in their writings. Some writers say that Emanuel Levinas's philosophy is a reaction to the holocaust; and there are some traces of the war horror Salinger witnessed in his short stories such as "For Esmé—with Love and Squalor."

In his book, Levinas describes the experience of becoming aware of a "call" for taking responsibility over other persons. According to Levinas, this *moral call* does not originate from sympathy, love, or even moral principles, but rather it's an

---

[1] *Totality and Infinity: An Essay on Exteriority*, Duquesne University Press, 1961.

inescapable feature of a face-to-face encounter with another person. The "catcher in the rye" motif itself is an expression of this moral call—taking responsibility for persons that you encounter—or catch—coming through "a big field of rye."

Social Reality as a War

Totality and Infinity begins by raising the question of whether we're duped by morality. We may be prone to think so, according to Levinas, in times of war and violence when the moral masks are taken down. Along the same lines, the *Realpolitik* approach in politics (also known as political realism) suggests that "moral principles" and "peace" are only verbal decorations beyond which the basic state of war still takes place. Peace is continuation of war by other means: there is a knife behind the diplomat's clean talk, and a perpetual battle of contradictory forces beneath the social organization of the state. *Totality and Infinity* is an attempt to resist this prevalent, yet disturbing picture.

Similarly, Holden suggests that society resembles a battlefield. Everywhere he turns, Holden sees people vigorously attempting to achieve their interests or to demonstrate superiority over others. The society of teenagers is an example. It's violent, sexually aggressive, and divided into groups that exclude the unpopular ones.

Holden suggests that the same "battlefield" situation, in a more sophisticated and implicit manner, exists in the adults' realm. Adults vigorously pursue status and power, but often conceal this (that is, they're "phonies"). The Headmaster of Elkton Hills changes his attitude towards the pupils' parents according to their social and economic status. Then there's Old Spencer, Holden's history teacher, who, in response to the headmaster's corny jokes, "practically kills himself choking and smiling and all" (22, p. 218). The same history teacher explains to Holden that life's a game that we should play according to the rules; Holden thinks to himself:

> Some game. If you get on the side where all the hot-shots are, then it's a game, all-right—I'll admit that. But if you get on the *other* side, where there aren't any hot-shots, then what's a game about it? Nothing. No game. (2, pp. 12–13)

Holden is well aware of the cynicism and the cruelty of the social "game" and therefore fantasies about running away in order to avoid participating in it.

This is the negative (or critical) side of Holden's view of the world. However, we may wonder whether Holden has something to offer; whether there's any positive or constructive side to Holden's approach to the world. Phoebe accuses Holden of thinking only in a negative way: he doesn't like anything that happens; he doesn't like schools and there is nothing he wants to be. However, I believe that Holden expresses a "moral call," namely, a response to the moral corruption he sees. This moral call is based upon a tacitly assumed world view or even a vision that can be uncovered by Levinas's philosophy.

The Awakening of an Ethical View

Levinas distinguishes between three ways of experiencing the world. One is characterized by *enjoyment* (or pain). The second is characterized by *labor and possession*. Both are egoistic in that they relate to the world merely as something that can supply the self with enjoyment and fulfill its needs.

The third one may help us to understand Holden's moral attitude. It is, first of all, characterized by *discourse*. In discourse, a person "manifests himself by proposing the world, by thematizing it" (p. 96). To thematize means to put things into categories with words. Words are generalizations; they present the individual thing (the "object") through its category, namely, the general group it belongs to, for example, this object in my hands becomes a "book," that creature rubbing against me trying to gain my attention becomes a "cat," as I sit here within a much larger object that is a "building."

Realization of the *other* person awakens in the self a new attitude towards the world: the ethical. The self feels committed to move beyond its purely egoistic relation to the world; it limits its pursuit of enjoyment and even the satisfaction of its needs in order to avoid damaging the other person. Moreover, the realization of the other person calls the self to take *responsibility* for the other person and to consider its needs. It is not the other person's power that causes the self to limit its egoistic drives, but rather the other person's weakness. In other words, it is the self's ability to hurt and even to murder the other person that may stop the self:

Conscience welcomes the Other. It is the revelation of a resistance to my powers that does not counter them as a greater force, but calls in question the naive right of my powers, my glorious spontaneity as a living being. Morality begins when freedom, instead of being justified by itself, feels itself to be arbitrary and violent. (p. 84)

The paradigmatic example of the *other* person that awakens the moral call is not someone that the self tends to like, but rather "the stranger, the widow and the orphan" (p. 77). What's more, the moral call, unlike pity, does not put the self in a higher position over the other person. On the contrary, although the other person might be poor and weak, the other person is—in a way—superior to the self, since encounters with the other person awakens a call to limit the self's egoism in order to secure justice for the other person.

Holden's Moral Attitude

Holden's moral attitude can be illuminated by drawing on what we've just discussed of Levinas's philosophy:

The Stranger, the Widow, and the Orphan

The episode in which Holden meets the two nuns shows Holden's moral attitude. The first thing to notice is Holden's kindness towards the nuns (the nuns are an embodiment of "the stranger, the widow and the orphan," at least for a secular adolescent). The second thing to notice is Holden's sensitivity to the nuns' economic status. He notices their inexpensive suticases and their meager breakfast: "All the two of them were eating for breakfast was toast and coffee. That depressed me. I hate it if I'm eating bacon and eggs or something and somebody else is only eating toast and coffee" (15, p. 143). A more mature person may take no notice of these things or just assume that economic gaps between people are natural ("that's the way the world is"). However, Holden, like a child, insists on questioning everything.

True Discourse

At the end of the conversation with the nuns Holden mentions that he's glad that the issue of religious affiliation never came up: "That's why I was glad those two nuns didn't ask me if I was a Catholic. It wouldn't have spoiled the conversation if they had, but it would've been different, probably. . . . All I'm saying is that it's no good for a nice conversation" (15, p. 147).

A distinction drawn by Levinas might explain why such talk doesn't make for "a nice conversation." Levinas distinguishes between *true* and *rhetoric* discourse. A true discourse is a face-to-face conversation in which we recognize the other person's uniqueness and avoid rhetoric discourse; that is, we don't approach the other person through strict categories (such as her or his social role, status, ethnic group, religious affiliation like Catholic, and so on) and avoid seeing them as an object for manipulation or control.

This may explain the oddity of Holden's fantasy of escaping from society. Holden is a very lonely protagonist (throughout his journey Holden yearns to have a true conversation with someone), but he's surrounded by a rhetoric (or phony) discourse in which people are often categorized and manipulated. So, one may say that Holden wishes to escape from the prevalent norms of rhetoric discourse, but not from having social interaction with other people, as long as it is honest.

Totality and Totalitarianism

Levinas criticizes the tendency of western thought to put everything under a unifying inclusive system and hence to view reality as a *totality* (for example, Plato's notion of reality as a system of ideas, of which the actual world is a pale shadow). Levinas's view has a political aspect: there is an association between totality and a tendency to totalitarianism, a tendency that could easily lead to abolition of the individual's uniqueness; Levinas expresses this notion with the term "the tyranny of the state" (p. 46).

Holden's non-conformism is close to Levinas's worry about totalitarianism. A revealing example is Holden's complaint about Mr. Vinson's oral expression class. In this class each pupil was required to make a speech, and once he digressed from the subject, all the other pupils were supposed to yell at him "digression!" Holden finds this procedure terrible:

. . . you're supposed to leave somebody alone if he's at least being interesting and he's getting all excited about something. I like it when somebody gets excited about something. It's nice. You just didn't know this teacher, Mr. Vinson. He could drive you crazy sometimes, him and goddam class. I mean he'd keep telling you to *uni*fy and *simpl*ify all the time. Some things you just can't do that to. I mean you can't hardly ever simplify and unify something just because somebody *wants* you to. (24, p. 240)

Mr. Vinson's pedagogic procedures and his requirement to simplify and unify is a good example of the "totalitarianism of the same," that is, the tendency to enforce inclusive uniformity. This may explains Holden's "surprising" decision to avoid Mr. Vinson's classes at the price of getting F in a subject in which he actually has quite good ability.

The Face

A prominent Levinasian theme is the moral significance of the face in our encounters with others: "The face is a living presence; it is expression . . . The face speaks" (p. 66). The face cannot be thematized within representation; instead, the face is a primordial expression of the uniqueness of the *other* person, that is, of its "being for itself." Levinas argues that the moral call is awakened once there is a face-to-face encounter with another person.

Holden also expresses a special attitude towards the faces of other persons, for example, when he explains why he disapproves of fist fights he says: ". . . what scares me most in a fist fight is the guy's face. I can't stand looking at the other guy's face, is my trouble. It wouldn't be so bad if you can both be blindfolded or something" (13, p. 117). The second reference to the face relates to a semi-sexual episode Holden witnesses; the man and woman squirting water or highballs out of their mouths at each other at the Edmont Hotel:

I think if you don't really like a girl, you shouldn't horse around with her at all, and if you *do* like her, then you're supposed to like her face, and if you like her face, you ought to be careful about doing crumby stuff to it, like squirting water all over it. (9, p. 81)

It seems that Holden's disturbed by this episode since he sees in it disrespect for the other person, in particular, a disrespect for another's uniqueness, which is most expressed by the face.

Holden's Attitude to Sex

I believe that Holden's hesitation in regard to sex is related to his moral attitude. The opposite approach to sex is presented by Stradlater, Holden's roommate at Pencey. Holden describes Strangler's approach with repulsion:

> What a technique that guy had. What he'd do was, he'd start snowing his date in this very quiet, *sincere* voice—like as if he wasn't only a very handsome guy but a nice, *sincere* guy, too. I damn near puked, listening to him. His date keeps saying, "No—*please*. Please, don't. *Please*." But old Stradlater kept snowing her in this Abraham Lincoln, sincere voice, and finally, there'd be this terrific silence in back of the car. (7, p. 64)

Stradlater uses rhetoric (or phony) discourse in order to achieve his sexual purpose.

When Stradlater dates a girl that Holden likes, Holden finds it terrible that Stradlater is not interested in knowing any details about her, for example, that she leaves all the kings in the back row of the checkers board; that is, Stradlater is not interested in all those practically trivial details that actually make her a unique person. He is interested in her only as a mere sexual object. His attitude resembles what James Barrel characterizes as the "objectifying attitude":

> We view the other as an object separate from and not embedded in the world. We see the body as consisting of parts; we see legs or breast rather than the total person. For the most part this objectifying gaze gives attention to the erogenous zones and body boundaries, avoiding the head and face. [2]

Holden finds it wrong to view another person as a sexual object. An illustrative example is Holden getting depressed rather than "sexy" when he meets a prostitute. The episode in which Holden hangs up the prostitute's dress in the closet is revealing:

> It was funny. It made me feel sort of sad when I hung it up. I thought of her going in a store and buying it, and nobody in the store knowing

---

[2] James Barrel, "Sexual Arousal in Objectifying Attitude," *Review of Existential Psychology and Psychiatry* 13:1 (1974), p. 99.

she was a prostitute and all. The salesman probably just thought she
was a regular girl when she bought it. It made me feel sad as hell—I
don't know. (13, p. 125)

Having sex with a prostitute is a good example of the "objectifying attitude." The prostitute means for the client "a body" or
"flesh," and the client means for the prostitute "money." The
participants in such an "interpersonal" interaction are wholly
defined for each other by the roles they are supposed to take in
it. There can't be any awareness of the other person's uniqueness if the interaction is to succeed. Hence, to think about a
prostitute in an ordinary situation (for example, as a woman
who goes out shopping for a dress) conflicts with the prostitute-
client interaction. Maybe Holden's lousy feeling and total lack
of desire to have sex with the prostitute are relatable to his
refusal to adopt the "objectifying attitude" towards the prostitute, which seems necessary for such a situation.

Taking Responsibility

Levinas's philosophy suggests that encounters with *another*
person call the self to limit its egoistic conduct in order to take
responsibility for her or him. The notion of responsibility
appears in the *Catcher* through the motif of the catcher in the
rye. The catcher in the rye is mentioned by Holden in his
description of a little boy walking with his parents:

> The cars zoomed by, brakes screeched all over the place, his parents
> paid no attention to him, and he kept on walking next to the curb and
> singing "If a body catch a body coming through the rye." It made me
> feel better. It made me feel not so depressed any more. (16, p. 150)

It seems that at this stage the catcher in the rye symbolizes the
fantasy of following one's inner voice and ignoring the external
alienating reality. Later, however, when Holden describes what
he likes to be, the catcher in the rye gets a different, almost
opposite, meaning:

> "Anyway, I keep picturing all these little kids playing some games in
> this big field of rye and all. Thousands of little kids, and nobody's
> around—nobody big, I mean—except me. And I'm standing on the

edge of some crazy cliff. What I have to do, I have to catch everybody if they start to go over the cliff—I mean if they're running and they do not look where they're going I have to come out from somewhere and *catch* them. That's all I'd do all day. I'd just be the catcher in the rye and all. I know it's crazy, but that's the only thing I'd really like to be. I know it's crazy." (22, pp. 224–25)

Here the catcher in the rye relates to responsibility; going outside of yourself and taking responsibility for another person is the basic landscape of Levinasian philosophy. Also, "to catch" has a double meaning; in addition to apprehend, "to catch" means to hold. So, catching someone implies that you've not only perceived her, but that you have become, at least to some degree, responsible for her (that is, holding her and preventing her from falling). We may then interpret the motif of the catcher in the rye as relating to the experience of a moral call to take responsibility over people one meets in the world ("this big field of rye").

Responsibility is also the key to the novel's ending. At the end of his journey Holden is very close to a mental and physical breakdown. In this sense the *Catcher* is like a thriller; the reader is anxious to find out what Holden is going to do to avoid the "fall" that Mr. Antolini warned him about. Holden, finally, decides to fulfill his fantasy of running away and living on the edge of society, pretending to be a deaf-mute, in order to escape the social "game." So, he decides to say goodbye to Phoebe. However, once he realizes that Phoebe has decided to escape with him, he changes his mind and decides to stay. The story ends with Holden watching Phoebe riding the carrousel. He feels so happy *then* that he almost cries out of happiness and relief.

Once Holden realizes the possible terrible effects on Phoebe of his running away, he decides to stay, that is, he takes responsibility. In the crossroads, between running away and staying, the moral call is crucial. Indeed, *The Catcher* is a novel about adolescence and the difficulty of becoming an adult person. Yet, the soul of the novel is morality. It presents the moral conflict that an adolescent is prone to experience once she or he realizes the moral corruption of society. On the one hand, the moral call makes it difficult for Holden to accept the norms of society and become part of it as an adult person; on the other hand, the moral call prevents Holden, at the end of the line, from running away from society.

Epilogue

Holden says that if you really love a book you feel that you'd like to give the author a call and be his friend. So, when I first read *The Catcher*, I felt that I'd like to give J.D. Salinger a call (today a reader might wish to send an email or to say hello through Facebook). When I thought about writing this chapter I imagined myself asking Salinger if Holden indeed was at the crossroads between taking responsibility and running away. I even thought of implying that, in a sense, Salinger himself has decided to run away. But that would have been too clever and coarse.

So, if I were able to call up old Salinger, I probably would thank him for writing this wonderful novel and for reminding us—the readers—about the basic moral call; a call that we may miss in the rush of life. That's, more or less, all I would want to say.[3]

---

[3] This essay is dedicated to the memory of my good friend Josef Horowitz with whom I read *Totality and Infinity* and other philosophical creations. I wish to thank Keith Dromm and Heather Salter for their editing.

8
Holden Onto What's Right

JAMIE CARLIN WATSON

Holden finds the world a very strange place. People live by, what seem to him, an odd set of rules: "It was the last game of the year, and you were supposed to commit suicide or something if old Pencey didn't win" (1, p. 5); "I'm always saying 'Glad to've met you' to somebody I'm not at all glad I met" (12, p. 114); ". . . it's really hard to be roommates with people if your suitcases are much better than theirs. . . . You think . . . that they don't give a damn whose suitcases are better, but they do" (15, 142); "Who wants flowers when you're dead? Nobody" (20, p. 201).

Holden also observes that people act as if you *should* obey these rules; there is apparently some sort of obligation to keep them. As old Spencer says, "Life *is* a game, boy. Life *is* a game that one plays according to the rules" (2, p. 12).

Holden thinks this is absurd: "Game, my ass. Some game. If you get on the side where all the hot-shots are, then it's a game, all right—I'll admit that. But if you get on the other side, where there aren't any hot-shots, then what's a game about it?" (2, p. 12). But he's not an anarchist; Holden does believe in rules. He even evaluates people's behavior, including his own, by a set of "principles" (13, p. 119).

So, what's the problem here? What are these rules that everyone else seems to think are so important, and why do they conflict with Holden's principles?

Three Types of Normativity

We all make judgments using the word "should." Philosophers call these *normative* judgments, and distinguish three types: social, legal, and moral.

Although Holden doesn't know much philosophy, he has an intuitive grasp of the differences between these concepts. He uses the word "phony" to describe people who treat a particular social norm—that of being accepted by others—as if it were a moral norm. He uses the word "bastard" to describe people who knowingly violate moral norms. And he uses the word "moron" to refer to people who are unable to make informed moral judgments. Holden's also painfully aware that he is unable to act according to moral norms, calling himself a "madman" when he discovers an inconsistency between his principles and his behavior. Holden is a moral agent trying very hard to do what he believes he *should* do.

Some Oughts and Shoulds

In *The Catcher in the Rye*, there is a tension between two types of normative claims. The first type involves claims about actions that *a lot of people think* other people ought or ought not do: you're "supposed" to take it personally if your home team doesn't win the big game; you "should" say "Glad to've met you" even when you're not; you "ought" to associate only with people from your own economic class; and you "should" send flowers to funerals. But if you violate one of these rules, it doesn't seem as if you've done something "wrong" or "immoral"; you just aren't following the crowd. Claims of this type are *social norms*.

The second type involves claims about what *people really* ought or ought not do: " . . . a guy like Morrow that's always snapping their towel at people's asses—really trying to hurt somebody with it . . . " (8, p. 74); "What you should be is not yellow at all" (13: 117); "I *don't* owe you five bucks" (14, p. 134); "I know I shouldn't have said it" (17, p. 173). If you violate one of these rules, it seems you aren't just going against the crowd; you're doing something really wrong—hurting someone, physically or emotionally, or taking something that rightfully belongs to him. These kinds of claims are *moral norms*.

There is a third type of normative claim to which Holden doesn't give much thought but—*because* he doesn't give it much thought—figures importantly in *Catcher*'s plot. These are norms explicitly dictated by people about what others should or should not do, and they are typically attended by some form of accountability, for example, a system of punishments for violations. These rules are *legal norms*.

Legal norms may have nothing to do with what people generally think (social norms) or morality (moral norms). They may be motivated solely by someone's interests, for example, a sign that says, "Parking for Vice President Only," or "No Smoking on Premises." Society may express no particular norm about the vice president's parking space or the general permissibility of smoking. Similarly, the motive for the signs may be practical, rather than moral—even if no one thought it immoral to smoke on the premises, they may still prefer not being around smoking. To be sure, legal norms *may* sometimes be derived from moral or social norms, for instance, "Murder is illegal" (moral) or "Men must remove hats in building" (social). Legal norms are unique in that they require that people publically identify them (for instance, in a rulebook, on a sign, in the written law) and that people hold others accountable for keeping or not keeping them (fines, expulsion, prison).

Some examples of legal norms in *The Catcher* include: "They kicked me out . . . on account of I was flunking four subjects" (1, p. 6); "You weren't allowed to smoke in the dorm" (6, p. 54); "I don't believe this is a smoker" (8, p. 72); "They lose their jobs if they get caught selling to a minor" (10, p. 91). In all these cases, someone has devised a set of rules and punishments for violating those rules. These examples are all legal norms even though the "law" involved in some cases is private, for instance, the grade and smoking rules at Pencey.

Holden's behavior highlights a distinction philosophers have made between claims about *personal preferences* and claims about *norms*. Traditional moral philosophers argue that moral claims express something about objective reality, reality independently of a person's preferences. Some moral philosophers have challenged the traditional view, arguing, instead, that moral claims are nothing more than expressions of what we prefer. If moral claims express truths at all, they express only subjective truths, in particular, truths about our tastes.

For instance, someone who holds this view might argue that the claim, "Murder is wrong," merely means, "Yuck, I don't like murder!" and the claim "Rape is immoral," simply means, "I feel a strong distaste for the act of rape."

This is not what people generally *think* they mean by moral claims; they think they are expressing objective moral truths. But these philosophers argue that people are expressing their feelings rather than making claims about reality. Since moral claims are merely "expressions" of preference or sentiment, this view is often called "Expressivism."

Though he is not always consistent, some of Holden's statements permit us to highlight this distinction between personal preference and genuine moral claims. Holden explicitly identifies some of his judgments as matters of taste. After leaving old Spencer's house, he comments, "I'd never yell 'Good luck!' at anybody. It sounds terrible, when you think about it" (2, p. 21). It may not be *wrong* to yell "Good luck!" at someone, and Holden seems to allow that Spencer's intentions may be good. Nevertheless, he thinks, personally, there is something distasteful about yelling it. Similarly, in reflecting on his conversation with the nuns, he notes, "I was glad those two nuns didn't ask me if I was a Catholic. . . . I'm not saying I *blame* Catholics. I don't. I'd be the same way, probably, if I was a Catholic" (15, p. 147).

He doesn't cast any "blame" on Catholics for wanting to know whether you're Catholic, but, as a matter of preference, he appreciated that the nuns didn't ask. Since Holden distinguishes at least some behaviors as distasteful but not immoral, and since, as we will see, he identifies at least some behaviors as immoral, we may presume that Holden does not consider himself an expressivist. And, in fact, Holden draws some fairly sophisticated distinctions among three categories of people that are more consistent with the traditional approach than with Expressivism, namely: phonies, bastards, and morons.

Phonies, Bastards, and Morons

Holden describes a lot of people as "phonies." What are the defining characteristics of a "phony"? We can draw a sketch of the concept using Holden's numerous examples. When he runs into Lillian Simmons, she says, "How marvelous to see you!"

but she really only wants to know about Holden's brother, D.B., so Holden explains, "Strictly a phony" (12: 113). When commenting on ministers, he says, ". . . they have all these Holy Joe voices when they start giving their sermons. . . . I don't see why the hell they can't talk in their natural voice." Holden explains, "They sound so phony when they talk" (14, p. 131). Twice, when someone uses the word "grand" to mean "nice" or "good," Holden says, "If there's one word I hate, it's grand. It's so phony" (15, p. 138). And during the intermission of the play he sees with Sally Hayes, he notes all the people "smoking their ears off and talking about the play so that everybody could hear and know how sharp they were." Holden tells us, "You never saw so many phonies in all your life" (17, p. 164).

What's the criticism here? The word itself seems to imply some disingenuousness, but of what sort? It doesn't seem to be simply that people are trying to be something they're not. Hopefully, we are all trying to be something we are not: smarter, stronger, faster, published, a better person, more trustworthy, more honest, bi-lingual, assistant professor instead of just a grad student, and so on. Even Holden wants to be something he isn't—his fantasy is to be the catcher in a big field of rye (22, p. 225). So it's not likely that Holden is criticizing people for wanting to be something they're not.

It's more likely that the criticism is that they are *acting like* something they're not in order to fit a general expectation. The criticism is about *the thing they want to be*, which seems to be, *accepted by others*. Phonies do what others expect them to do, for instance, they say things like "How marvelous to see you!" when they don't exactly mean it, and "Grand!" and speak in Holy Joe voices, and talk so that others will know how "sharp" they are.

The problem is that, while there doesn't seem to be any moral obligation to be what others want you to be, these people act as if there were. And they regard people negatively who do not attempt to be acceptable to others. Phonies treat the *social* norm of being accepted by others as if it were a *moral* norm, that is, they regard breaking social norms as *deserving moral blame*.

Holden's criticism doesn't imply that the desire to be accepted is inherently immoral. None of the actions mentioned above seem to have anything to do with what's morally right or wrong. And the desire for acceptance is not, in itself, essentially impermissible, permissible, or obligatory. There may be cases when it is permissible and cases when it isn't; or there may be cases when it is obligatory and cases when it isn't. So, the moral criticism seems to be just that some people act as if social norms were moral norms—they *conflate* the two. And, in Holden's opinion, this warrants some degree of moral blame. People should know better. Even if a particular phony act is not immoral, according to Holden, it is irresponsible to regard something as an obligation that isn't.

We get a clearer picture of his willingness to blame phonies in a case where he suspends it because of a mitigating condition. Holden says that Ernie, the piano player, acts like a phony, but that he can't blame him because "I don't even think he *knows* any more when he's playing right or not. It isn't all his fault. I partly blame all those dopes that clap their heads off—they'd foul up *any*body, if you give them a chance" (12, p. 110). Ernie is not officially a phony, or at least no longer one, because he's conditioned by other phonies. It would seem that continual phoniness can eventually undermine your and others' ability to make morally responsible decisions. Therefore, according to Holden, if you are morally responsible for your actions, you have a moral obligation not to be phony. Ernie seems to have lost the ability to draw the distinction.

In addition to phonies, Holden calls a lot of people "bastards." He is much clearer about what he means by this term, telling us in Chapter 18 that a bastard is someone who's "very mean, or very conceited" (18, p. 176). The cases where he applies the term consistently reflect this definition. Old Stradlater is "too conceited" to rile up easily, disrespectful of other people's possessions (he stretches out Holden's jacket, 4, p. 44), and he uses Holden to write his English paper for him (Chapters 4–6). Holden calls him a "bastard" several times. Ernest Morrow tried to hurt people with his towel just for fun; Holden says he "was doubtless the biggest bastard that ever went to Pencey" (8, p. 71). The people in Ernie's bar are so conceited that, while they know they are taking up someone else's space, they don't move out of the way; Holden notes, "and they never *do*, the bastards" (12, p. 111). Al Pike is "All muscles and no brains" who "thought he was very hot stuff." And while Jane Gallagher says he has an inferiority complex, Holden says he's a "show-off bastard."

As with phonies, these cases also have moral implications, but of a slightly more nefarious sort. Being mean to someone, that is, causing either physical or emotional harm without sufficient cause, is generally regarded as immoral. Being "conceited" is less obviously immoral, though we can imagine that conceit often motivates harmful behavior, such as emotional abuse or disregard for others' property. But it is important to note that all of Holden's examples reflect this moral dimension of his definition. It would seem then, that "bastards," as Holden applies the term, are people who violate moral norms. They're worse than phonies because, while they aren't necessarily acting to be accepted by others, they aren't even trying to be something they are *morally obligated* to be.

A few people in Holden's life are both "phonies" and "bastards." These concepts are not mutually exclusive, that is, they can both be true of someone. If a person conflates social norms with moral norms and also violates moral norms, she is both a phony and a bastard. His former headmaster, Haas, at the Elkton Hills school is "the phoniest bastard I ever met in my life" (2, p. 19). At the Sunday dinners, when families were invited, Haas would be "charming as hell" and smile a phony smile at the "old funny-looking parents," then spend time with parents who were more socially acceptable. Haas was a phony because he preferred the socially acceptable people over the funny-looking people, and he was a bastard because this was an overtly hurtful thing to do. "George something" from Andover college is also both a phony and a bastard. He has a phony way of stepping back to answer a question, and he has "one of those very phony, Ivy League voices, one of those very tired, snobby voices" (17, p. 166) (I imagine Counselor Mackey from *South Park*, "Mmmkay?" or *Family Guy*'s Mr. Bottomtooth). But he's a bastard because he tries to "horn in" on Holden's date (17, p. 166).

There are a few characters in *The Catcher in the Rye* that, though they often act like phonies or bastards or both, Holden doesn't call them by these names or regard them with the same contempt. For instance, the three girls at the Lavender Room act like phonies and bastards. "The blonde" he dances with tells him she saw Peter Lorre last night, "The movie actor. In person," and then tells him to watch his language. But instead of calling her a phony (because society says you're supposed to revere movie stars and not use foul language in public), he calls her a "moron" (10, p. 93).

What's the difference between a phony and a moron? Apparently, intelligence. "They didn't invite me to sit down at their table—mostly because they were too ignorant. . . . You could hardly tell which was the stupidest of the three of them" (10, p. 95). Two of the girls were drinking Tom Collinses in December, which, apparently, is a social *faux pas*, but Holden explains that, "They didn't know any better" (10, p. 97).

The girls also acted like bastards. They had ordered drinks before Holden showed up, but they left him with the whole tab. "I think they should've at least *of*fered to pay for the drinks they had before I joined them. . . ." (10, p. 98). Their not offering is not merely a violation of a social norm; they incurred the cost of their earlier drinks and Holden had no moral obligation to pay for them. In stiffing him for those drinks, they were, in essence, stealing from him. But instead of calling them bastards, Holden says, "I didn't care much, though. They were so ignorant" (10, p. 98). Here, as with "phony," the difference between being a bastard and being a moron, is intelligence. They couldn't have known better.

Why might a person's ignorance mitigate Holden's judgment about her? There is a well-respected principle in moral philosophy called "ought implies can." The idea is that there can be no obligation for you do something that you cannot do. For instance, you could not have a moral obligation to jump over a building or to fly by flapping your wings because, physically, you can't do either. Similarly, if you do not have the mental capacity for making moral decisions, it would be mistaken to hold you responsible for those decisions. This's why we do not hold infants or people with severe mental disabilities morally responsible for crimes—literally, they could not know any better. Holden seems to regard the ladies in Lavender Room as mentally incompetent to make informed moral decisions. Therefore, the terms "phony" and "bastard" just don't apply.

How should we respond to "morons"? Not with moral blame; they do not have the intelligence required for understanding most moral norms. Consistent with the "ought implies can" principle, Holden seems to think the only legitimate response is to become "depressed" or to "feel sorry" for these people. Holden seems to blame Ernie the piano player for being a snob and a phony, but on reflection, he decides that Ernie might not be responsible for his phoniness (because he has been manipulated by all the phonies in the crowd). After this, Holden just "felt sort of sorry for him" (12, p. 110).

The Catchers

In addition to phonies, bastards, and morons, Holden identifies another type of person that is more idealistic. These people are morally responsible for their actions; they're not trying to impress anyone, conflating social norms with moral norms; they're not violating any moral norms; and they exhibit some form of moral virtue. These are the "catchers" of the story. Holden doesn't actually call anyone a "catcher," but a "catcher in the rye," a person protecting children from a metaphorical cliff, is his moral ideal (22, p. 225). Catchers are unique because they either generally do the right thing or are generally honest with themselves about who they should be.

Holden's history teacher "old Spencer" is a catcher because, though he uses the word "grand" like a phony, he was fair in grading Holden's paper and he genuinely cares about him. He treats Holden with respect, challenges him about his future, offers him hot chocolate, and wishes him good luck (though Holden doesn't appreciate the latter). In addition, Holden's conversation with Spencer highlights the distinction Holden recognizes between moral norms and personal preferences. Though Holden doesn't consider Spencer a phony, bastard, or moron, he constantly complains about the man's demeanor: that his room smells like Vicks Nose Drops, his "sad, ratty old bathrobe" (2, p. 11), his nodding all the time (p. 12), his picking his nose (p. 13), that he read Holden's paper to him aloud (p. 16), and that he yelled "good luck" to him as he went out the door (p. 21). Holden seems to think old Spencer is morally responsible for his actions, is a pretty "nice old guy" (2, p. 12), yet he doesn't like how the man presents himself. Holden consistently distinguishes his personal preferences from his moral judgments.

Mr. Antolini, Holden's former English teacher at Elkton Hills, could have been a catcher because, despite what anyone thinks of him, he consistently (for a while) does the right thing. He was the only one who cared about James Castle (who jumped out the window, 22, p. 221); he checked to see whether he was still alive and took him to the infirmary (23, p. 226). He also seemed to care genuinely about Holden. Even though Holden is no longer his student, or even at Elkton Hills, Antolini listens to Holden's problems, allows him to stay in his home, and challenges him to be a better student and person. But then he starts "being perverty" and Holden leaves (24, p. 249). Holden's impression of Antolini and Antolini's "pervert" behavior confuses Holden, and he doesn't know what to think about him—whether he's a caring person who likes to touch people, or whether he's really a pervert (25, p. 253).

But the catcher most important to Holden, the character who can do no wrong in his eyes, is his sister, Phoebe. Phoebe is sharp; she's "Somebody with sense and all"; "she knows exactly what the hell you're talking about"; she can tell the difference between a good movie and a bad one, which is important to Holden; she's passionate, particularly about writing (something all the Caulfields seem to have in common and which Holden respects a great deal) (10, p. 88); "she always listens when you tell her something" (22, p. 218); when Holden tells her he's broke, she gives him all her Christmas money, and she puts her arm around his neck until he stops crying (23, pp. 232–33). Phoebe is a class act, plus she can dance. Phoebe is a catcher, because all of these character traits motivate Holden to be a better person. She is just what he needs her to be when he needs it the most—therefore, she saves him from the cliff. Phoebe may even be the reason Holden doesn't run away, though it's equally plausible that it is his own weakness of will.

Holden is noticeably absent from the list of catchers. He hasn't yet achieved his moral ideal; though being a catcher in the rye is the only thing he'd really like to be (22, p. 225). This raises a question about where Holden sees himself in relation to these other characters.

Holden the Madman

Holden doesn't consistently claim for himself any of these former titles in his value scheme. He sometimes calls himself a bastard, or admits to doing phony things, and he certainly doesn't identify himself with the catchers. Holden finds his own behavior inconsistent with his beliefs, and in several places we find him floundering in moral indecision, trying to do what's right, but often falling short. He explicitly admits that he's a liar: "I'm the most terrific liar you ever saw in your life" (3, p. 22). Though he regularly makes sex rules for himself, he keeps breaking them (9, p. 82); he apologizes for using foul language, consenting to regard at least this social norm as a moral norm (10, p. 95); he tells us he is deficient in the virtue of courage (13, pp. 116–17); though it is against his principles, he agrees to pay a prostitute to come to his room (13, p. 119); and he yawns in the middle of Mr. Antolini's lecture, calling himself a *"rude bastard"* (24, p. 247).

While he is conscious of both moral and social norms, he violates the former and sometimes treats the latter as the former. And he experiences some degree of psychological conflict over this. But unlike phonies and bastards, Holden tries to do better—he refuses to be in a movie short to avoid being a phony (11, p. 100); he hides his more expensive luggage under his bed so as not to exacerbate his roommate Slagle's insecurity (15, p. 141); and he gives money to the nuns because he thinks it's the right thing to do (15, p. 143).

Holden apparently finds the inconsistency between his bad and good behavior strange and unfortunate, because many of these instances are punctuated with him calling himself "crazy" or "a madman." This introduces a whole new category into our scheme, though, like Holden himself, it is difficult to align with the others. When one of the girls at the Lavender Room tells him to stop using foul language, he apologizes "like a madman," though he doesn't mean it (10, p. 95). When he mistakenly blows smoke in the nuns' faces, he apologizes "like a madman" (15, p. 147)—and while accidents are not regularly considered moral infractions, Holden's embarrassment is enough to make him doubt his morality. When he tells Sally he loves her, but cannot say whether it is really a lie, he says, "I'm crazy. I swear to God I am" (17, p. 163). He tells Sally she's a pain in the ass, and, while he knows he shouldn't have said it, he is not really sorry he did. Nevertheless, he apologizes, "like a madman" (17, p. 173). And finally, he recognizes that his drunk call to Sally in the middle of the night to make amends for hurting her feelings was not a good idea: "When I'm drunk, I'm a madman" (20, p. 197).

As Holden wades through the consequences of flunking out of Pencey, he seems to find it easy to label the rest of the world according to a clear set of moral standards, but finds trouble when he examines his own behavior. "Madman" seems to operate like a moral placeholder until he develops a stronger will to do what's right. It's likely that, in his immaturity, he doesn't realize the complexities of the human condition and that the people he meets are likely just as inconsistent as he is. It's possible that he has some slight awareness of this, since he vacillates between judging a particular *action* to be phony and judging particular *people* to be phonies. Perhaps as he develops morally, he will begin to see this distinction clearly, and thereby relieve some of his frustration at himself.

While Holden's judgments are generally immature and his attitude wanting in sophistication, his ability to trace clearly the outlines of moral concepts is somewhat impressive. With a bit of motivation, a touch of humility, and continuing interaction with the catchers in his life, he may grow up to be a catcher in the rye after all.[1]

---

[1] Thanks to Tim Moore at Young Harris College for the idea of using the term "catchers" for the good characters in the story.

Where Do the Ducks Go?

9
The Elderly Teenager

Marcus Schulzke

Holden Caulfield is both obsessed with time and oblivious to it. Throughout *The Catcher in the Rye*, he is persistently analyzing people and making judgments based on their age. At times, he even seems to think that age determines the way people think.

He is also intensely fascinated by youth and by anything that seems ageless. He is drawn to the Museum of Natural History, especially the mummies because they are mysterious, enduring relics from the past. He loves children because they represent genuine feelings, as opposed to adult phoniness. He is also oblivious to time as it relates to his own life. He's continually frustrating other people with his inability to plan—or even to know what time of day it is.

Holden's strange relation to time is part of what makes him such a compelling character. It makes him unusual and sets him apart from others. Yet what makes him interesting to the reader is also what makes him so frustrating for the book's other characters. His strange relation to time may be the source of his angst and is certainly at the root of many of his strained relationships.

Holden tries to arrest change. He becomes obsessed with what appears to be stationary and values it above all else. He is drawn to everything static. But he can never actually succeed in stopping time. His attempts to hold onto the past and the present, to avoid thinking about the future as anything fundamentally different from the present, inevitably fail. As we're all painfully aware, time cannot be halted. We can never prevent things around us from changing, or even hold onto the moments we value most. This is a lesson we learn early in life, but Holden refuses to accept it.

Although the novel ends with a change in Holden's outlook, during most of it Holden experiences a contest between two different philosophical views about *time*. Holden has little appreciation of academics, and says nothing at all about philosophy, but if he had studied the subject, he would have seen that his interest in time was not unique. The conflict he experiences lies at the roots of Western philosophy. By looking back on the ancient Greek philosophers Heraclitus and Parmenides, who presented two extreme views of how things change or fail to change over time, we can better understand Holden's divided self.

Holden attempts to impose the Parmenidean view of the world as Being onto what he fearfully perceives is a Heraclitian world of Becoming. Parmenides thinks all change is illusory and that the world is essentially timeless. Heraclitus, by contrast, argues that there is only change; no experience can ever be repeated or preserved. Holden can find no point of stability, no reconciliation like that provided by Plato's theory of the forms. He is caught between two incompatible views of the world and tries to transform his own identity into something essential and unchanging.

Perception of Time

Holden does not try to understand time on a philosophical level. He's only concerned with it as a practical matter. Yet his perception is at odds with the way time is commonly perceived. Most people are aware of their existence in what the American philosopher William James (1842–1910) called a "specious present."[1] This is the short period of time that we think of as being "now." It is the moment we exist in, but even while in the present, our thoughts are constantly shifting back and forth between it, the past, and the future.

We use our present to reflect on what we have done and to plan for the future. We often lose our connection with the pre-

---

[1] William James. *The Principles of Psychology: Volume 1*, Holt, 1918, p. 606.

sent as our thoughts take us elsewhere. This can flatten out the perception of time, making the past and future seem like they exist in the present. James and others reach the conclusion that the present is really an irreducible instant, a point in time that has no duration. It's entirely constructed out of the future and the past. This is an idea with a long history. Saint Augustine even argues that no one can seriously doubt this truth.[2] He thinks that our perception of the present is just a combination of memories and expectations.

For Holden, someone who seems to have no expectations, explaining the present in this way is inadequate. He lives in a world of memories imposed on the present, with little attention to how the things he remembers have changed. The most obvious sign of this is Holden's strange behavior.

Throughout the story, Holden has no sense of time. Others must remind him of how blatantly he upsets their schedules. On the train, he tries to go to the dining car when it's closed, with apparently no sense of when normal people would be eating (8, p. 75). When he arrives in New York, he calls Faith Cavendish and pressures her to go out even though it's too late (9, p. 85). Later in the book he calls Sally and speaks to her grandmother, who asks him if he knows what time it is; he ignores the question (20, p. 195). Holden's not stupid. He knows that others find his behavior odd and that he's breaking with convention by calling people late at night. He's aware of time, and how much it governs other people's lives, he just tries very hard to ignore it.

This becomes even more extreme when he tells Sally about his plan to leave the city, a plan that must be enacted right at that moment (17, p. 171). It can't wait for the future that Holden ignores. When Holden first meets Sally for their date, he seems to be a normal teenager. He is, in his own cynical way, concerned about her enjoying the date and liking him. As their relationship builds throughout the date, Holden attempts to pull her into his world of Being by asking her to leave with him. She refuses since she can't accept his neglect for future concerns. Holden refuses to consider life being any different in the future, except insofar as it might be weighed down by all the things that make a person phony if he succumbs to the

---

[2] Saint Augustine. *Confessions*, Kessinger, 1942, pp. 260–64.

ordinary view of the world. Delaying the trip is a threat to his identity so he reacts violently. From this, we can see that Holden does understand the way others perceive time and how much he hates it. They see the inevitability of change and organize their lives around it. They tacitly accept Heraclitus's theory of Becoming.

The Stationary World

Parmenides lived shortly after Heraclitus, during the early fifth century B.C. Parmenides takes a much different perspective on the nature of the world than Heraclitus, one that emphasizes stability rather than change. He argues that things are either existent or nonexistent, Being or Nonbeing. Something cannot really be half-alive; it can only be alive or dead. There are no partial states; everything either is or is not. Anything that exists is entirely existent and anything that does not exist is absent from the world. If there are only the two states of Being and Nonbeing, then there cannot be any degrees of Being. This means that there cannot be any decay or entropy, since this would imply a reduction of Being. By the same standard, there cannot be growth or development, since these categories imply an increase in Being. Not only can things not change state, motion itself is nonexistent. The conclusion this leads to is that the world and the things in it never change. There is only Being, never Becoming.

Parmenides's theory leads us to the counterintuitive notion that everything that exists is in an unalterable state of Being. He reaches this conclusion deductively, by starting at the metaphysical level and then using it to explain everyday life, while Heraclitus seems to be working in the opposite direction, inductively. Parmenides not only disagrees with Heraclitus's theory of time but also with his way of doing philosophy. He considers the idea that we cannot step in the same river twice an example of our senses deceiving us about the way the world really is. He would warn us against Heraclitus's reliance on our senses and recommend the use of reason alone.

The Unstable World

Although little is known about Heraclitus, he seems to have been an outsider in the emerging community of ancient Greek philosophers, perhaps even somewhat like Holden himself. He did, after all, accuse the philosopher and mathematician Pythagoras of being a fraud (read: phony) and criticize the poets Xenophanes and Hectatus for learning a great deal without understanding anything.[3] However, he would certainly find much to hate if he were aware of Heraclitus's philosophy.

Many philosophers before and since Heraclitus have been interested in the way the world changes over time, but few have approached the subject from such a humanistic perspective. As an outsider, who seems to have been mostly self-taught, Heraclitus was able to think about problems in a different way than other philosophers. Time is usually the object of abstract speculation, and not approached as something belonging to lived experience. Many even doubt the power of the senses to tell us anything accurately. Yet Heraclitus based his work heavily on perception. This reflects Heraclitus' overriding concern with human experience.

Like Holden, Heraclitus is a skeptical and somewhat cynical judge of people, who is nevertheless fascinated by them. However, unlike Holden, he is deeply interested in change. So much so that he regards fire as the fundamental element. Fire is constantly moving, and changing the state of everything it touches. It may destroy what it touches, but in doing so, it also creates the foundation for something new: "All things exchange for fire and fire for all things, as goods are exchanged for gold and gold for goods" (p. 45). Heraclitus's world is one of constant Becoming; existence is never stationary.

Heraclitus's humanistic, common-sense understanding of the world is closely related to his theory of time. He insists that we do most of our thinking by relying on our senses and following their guidance. This's why so many of his thoughts seem to be based on observations of the natural world. He draws on events to reach more abstract truths. Many of his metaphors for explaining time reflect this. Heraclitus's most famous claim actually comes from Plato. *Cratylus* quotes Heraclitus as saying that we can't step into the same river twice.[4] Heraclitus argues

---

[3] Richard G. Geldard, *Remembering Heraclitus,* Lindisfarne, 2000, p. 130.
[4] Plato, *Cratylus*, Loeb, 1953, 402a.

that everything is in flux; nothing can happen twice. With the world constantly changing, we can't duplicate experiences, nor can we hold onto the past. No experience, even if it is as trivial as stepping into a river, can be repeated, as all the things that made the experience possible are unstable. Although Holden is vaguely aware of things changing, he is deeply troubled by experiences that confirm Heraclitus's theory of Becoming.

Mummies and Baseball Gloves

The theory of radical change serves a deeper purpose, since it allows Heraclitus to show that opposites are inseparable. One contrary must replace the other. Day and night, for example, are linked by their succession. They continually replace each other, and are only found as a pair. The same is true of death replacing life. This happens everywhere, except in the objects that Holden loves. Holden's obsession with static Being is made clear by his attraction to objects that symbolize stasis. When he is confused or unsure of himself, Holden turns to one of these objects and finds support in it. His hat, his baseball glove, and the mummies at the Museum of Natural History are a few of the objects he latches onto as a way of fighting change. They seem to defy the logic of Heraclitus's argument, since they are not like night and day; they are eternally in one state.

Holden reveals his fascination with mummies early in the book. After an entire semester of history, the only thing he considered worth remembering was about mummies. He's so amazed by them that he writes about nothing but mummies on his history exam (2, p. 16). Holden's disdain for history and love of mummies is revealing. Few subjects are more antithetical to Holden's view of the world than one that is often concerned with change over time. Many historians assume the Heraclitian view and describe history as a sequence of events that unfold over time. Describing history in terms of change is a threat to Holden's identity and leads him to despise everything about the subject, except for the stories about the Egyptians who attempted to preserve themselves forever.

Mummies are unchanging in a way that seems magical. Even modern science, which has solved countless puzzles, is powerless to discover how the mummies were made (2, p. 16). Mummies challenge the common-sense understanding of the world, even its highest expression, science. The fact that the mummies' secret to longevity cannot be understood makes them even more compelling, since Holden is in search of something so powerful that it can contradict what his senses tell him. Near the end of the book, he finds two boys who are curious about the museum's mummies (25, p. 263). He's eager to take them to the mummies, since seeing the mummies might provide him a sense of comfort and contact with the past. They do this, at least for him. The boys are frightened. They realize that the mummy is a dead body. Its stability does not change the fact that the body represents death. They are, like most people, curious and repulsed by the idea of achieving permanence if the only way to obtain it is through denying your own power to change.

Allie's baseball glove is an even more powerful symbol of permanence. The mummies are public, on display for everyone to see. The baseball glove is unique and therefore more authentic for Holden. When someone dies, their friends and family often try to remember them in objects. Keeping the glove as a reminder of Allie is a way of keeping him alive. His body cannot be saved like the mummies, but Holden manages to keep his memory alive and to remember his brother exactly as he was in a perfect moment. At times, he tries to show others the power of this symbol, such as when he writes about it for Stradlater's English essay, but they cannot understand the emotional value of the glove.

The same is true of the red hunting hat, but its meaning is very different than that of the mummies and the baseball glove. It's not only something unchanging and unique, it's also Holden's personal sign of individuality. No one has a hat like it, so it marks Holden out as an individual and serves as a stable reference point in a way that a glove belonging to his brother or a stranger's preserved body cannot. It connects Holden to his childhood. By doing this, the hat keeps Holden attached to a stationary identity that is based in memory. It stabilizes Holden's own identity just as the glove does for his brother's.

Still, Holden is embarrassed by the hat. It marks him out as being different from everyone else. He's especially concerned about it whenever he has to pretend to be older than he is. He occasionally sets aside this connection to his childhood, but keeps it close, and returns to it as soon as he can. Through these and other symbols, Holden makes his resistance to Heraclitus's world of becoming clear. He affirms it to the reader and to himself, even though both know that his resistance will not change anything. The world he attempts to create is the world of static Being, the one that another Greek philosophers, Parmenides, proposed.

The War Within

If Holden simply sided with Heraclitus or with Parmenides then he might be able to calmly live his life without any concern with philosophy. This is certainly what he wants to do. He wants to wholeheartedly endorse the Parmenidean theory and live a life that supports this view. Yet he cannot bring himself to believe that there is no change. His interest in the world as it appears leads him to see the world as Heraclitus does even though he resists this by hiding from any signs of change. He's torn between the Heraclitian and Parmenidean world views.

Holden's attention to human affairs leads him to trust his senses. Even his personality leads him towards Heraclitus, but his obsession with preventing change shows a powerful desire to side with Parmenides. Parmenides's philosophy seems much better, but he cannot succeed in detaching himself from the daily events that show evidence of change.

Much of Holden's internal crisis is due to the conflict between the conception of time that he wants to endorse and the one that's thrust upon him. He tries to stop moving forward, to freeze things as they are, or even to regress to an earlier time, but he knows that this is impossible. Every time he tries to live in the past or hold onto the present as a moment of stability, other characters intervene. Sometimes characters thwart his efforts to live only in the present or the past by insisting to him that he must change his life. More often other characters don't need to do or say anything; their very existence is a reminder of the stages of life that Holden must go through.

The Gray-Haired Teenager

One of the book's earliest clues about Holden's concern with aging is his reflection on the Spencers. He views the old couple with derisive pity and confesses that he thinks about Mr. Spencer often. Primarily, Holden wonders "what the heck he was still living for" (2, p. 11). He sees old age as a terrible state of physical ailments and strange interests. He seems to care about the Spencers, but he clearly has no desire to emulate them.

He likes Mr. Spencer as a person, but he hates what he represents. Holden shifts from describing the man to describing in general terms what he hates about old people: "I don't much like to see old guys in their pajamas and bathrobes anyway. Their bumpy old chests are always showing. And their legs. Old guys' legs, at beaches and places, always look so white and unhairy" (2, p. 11). He reacts similarly to many of the adults in the book, for example, the sixty-five-year-old bellboy at the Edmont Hotel, who he describes as "even more depressing than the room" (9, p. 80).

Holden's feelings about old age are emphasized by his interest in children. The alienated and cynical boy seems to have a great deal of compassion for those younger than him. This is clear in his descriptions of Phoebe and Allie, but he is even uncharacteristically considerate of children he does not know. He is outraged by anything that threatens to pull children out of their youth and expose them to the horrors of the adult world. One of his most emotional moments is his reaction to seeing "fuck you" written near his sister's school (25, p. 260):

> I kept wanting to kill whoever'd written it. I figured it was some perverty bum that'd sneaked in the school late at night to take a leak or something and then wrote it on the wall. I kept picturing myself catching him at it, and how I'd smash his head on the stone steps till he was good and goddam dead and bloody. (25, p. 261)

His reaction shows his desire to be the catcher in the rye and to protect the children from facing the world of adult things that he is afraid of.

Holden even has a strong desire to preserve the youth of those who are no longer children. This is why he is so shocked and angered by Stradlater's date with Jane Gallagher (6, p. 56). Holden imagines his childhood friend Jane being misled and exploited by Stradlater and tries to hold onto the relationship he had with her years earlier. It appears that he did not do much to preserve that relationship, but he insists on remembering the girl as she was when he was younger. He thinks of her as though she did not age. The illusion is so powerful that she never actually appears in the story and Holden refrains from using his opportunity to see her. To meet her again would mean shattering that illusion of her being exactly the same as he remembered. Stradlater threatens to do this when he forces Holden to think about Jane as being a sexual object. Holden's violent reaction to Stradlater shows how important it is for him to resist those who force change upon him.

The Heraclitian and Parmenidean worldviews even compete to define Holden's physical appearance and personality. He occupies an uncomfortable position between youth and adulthood. Holden tells the reader directly that he's sixteen, but even with this number explicitly stated, Holden's age is ambiguous. He looks old, acts young, enjoys adult settings, and hates the world adults occupy. He hires prostitutes and goes to bars, but cries when he is in danger and questions Old Luce about what mature experiences are really like. His body shows the signs of his divided identity. Perhaps the most prominent and feared sign of old age is gray hair, and he has had "millions of gray hairs" since he was very young (2, p. 13). With this and his height, Holden appears older than sixteen. Yet he admits to acting as if he were only twelve or thirteen and his friends seem to think that he acts much younger than he is. There is a vast disconnect between how he looks, how he acts, and how old he actually is. Even though we know his age, it does not categorize him.

Plato's Compromise

It's common for histories of philosophy to give Plato the credit for resolving the conflict between Heraclitus and Parmenides with his theory of the Forms. According to Plato, the world is both changing and stationary because there are really two worlds: a world of Being and a world of Becoming. We inhabit the world of Becoming. It's as we see it and requires no explanation.

The world of Being is apart from the one we inhabit and is made up of Forms. These Forms correspond to things in the world of Becoming, but they never enter that world. They are essences that give things in our world their shape. For example, Plato would say that the only reason we are able to identify different people as being human is that they all share some human essence that is deeper than any single person, or even all people put together. We might think of this as a human nature that all people embody. The idea of human nature is familiar, but Plato goes much further. He argues that everything in the world has an essence. There is an essence of tableness and chairness, just as there is an essence of humanness. The essences are unchanging and they are more real than any objects in the world. The world of essences is a Parmenidean world of Being; the world we experience is a Heraclitian world of Becoming.

By introducing a theory of two worlds, Plato can say that Parmenides and Heraclitus are each partially right. The former identifies the world of essences; the latter correctly describes the world we experience. Plato realizes that most people will be unable to accept this. He believes that only a philosopher (that is, one who believes in his philosophy) is capable of thinking in terms of the two world model, which means that only philosophers will be capable of truly understanding how misguided our ordinary understanding of time is. The ideal city Plato describes in the *Republic* is even constructed so as to detach the philosophers as much as possible from the world's superficial transformations. They live isolated and simple lives with no luxury. They are allowed to leave the world of Becoming, as much as a person can hope to, in order to live in a world without change.

Holden seems a perfect candidate for becoming a Platonic philosopher. Although his narrative is often cynical and lacks nuance, Holden does have the critical, reflective attitude of a Platonic philosopher. He stands aloof from the world, is conscious of this distance, and uses his position as a vantage point from which to contemplate everything he sees. Holden has the personality of such a philosopher, but as privileged as he is, he cannot remove himself from the world as completely as Plato would want. They must be able to leave the world of Becoming and live a life of reflection on the world of Being, but Holden cannot. When he tries, we see that he is too loyal to his sister to take this final step toward isolation. He must find a different kind of reconciliation between Heraclitus and Parmenides.

Moving Forward

The museum connects Holden to Phoebe and to his own past. He has fond memories of going to the museum when he was a kid and reflects on his sister going there with her class. When he meets his sister there, he seems to want the museum to be their final meeting place because it reinforces his wish to stop time by making the present identical to the past:

> I kept walking and walking, and I kept thinking about old Phoebe going to that museum on Saturdays the way I used to. I thought how she'd see the same stuff I used to see, and how she'd be different every time she saw it. (13, p. 117)

However, she refuses to let him leave alone and manages to bring him to the zoo, where Holden undergoes what seems to be a subtle transformation in his understanding of time.

When Phoebe stretches to take the golden ring on the car-rousel, we see that she's someone unafraid to hope for something and take some risks in order to achieve it. Watching her has a powerful effect on Holden. He realizes that part of being young is hoping that things will change and trying to direct that change in a favorable way. This makes him more comfort-able with the prospect of change in his own life. This brief scene and his conversation with Phoebe lead Holden to make one more attempt at living the life everyone wants him to have. At the end of the story, Holden reflects on how much he misses everyone. His unpleasant experience is transformed into a pleasant memory of a past that he cannot return to. However, he says that he should not tell anyone the story in order to avoid missing everyone. This is far from a clear resolution of Holden's inner conflict, but it seems to show that he is at least willing to try living with some attention to the future and accept that things must change.

10
The Sickness unto Barfing

DALE JACQUETTE

I'm just going through a phase right now. Everybody goes through phases and all, don't they? (2, pp. 20–21)

Holden Caulfield, the youthful narrator of J.D. Salinger's classic American novel of existential despair, *The Catcher in the Rye*, is profoundly disgusted with almost everyone he knows, with life in general, and especially with himself.

Most people feel disgusted with something or other at various times, which in small doses, depending on the circumstances, is sometimes experienced as an almost daily occurrence. What makes Holden's case different is the degree of his obsession. He suffers excessively from this ordinary emotional response to what many persons would likely find repulsive, if they paid as much attention as Holden does, turning with abhorrence from one revolting scene and situation to another. Holden dwells almost lovingly on the things that disgust him, describing them lavishly and in intimate detail.

What does *disgust* mean and why is Holden's urban odyssey so marked by such frequent distinctive loathing and revulsion? Holden is sick at heart, and as we read Salinger's novel, we must wonder why. His is not the nineteenth-century Danish philosopher Søren Kierkegaard's description of a *Sickness unto Death*, in his book of 1849, subtitled *A Christian Psychological Exposition for Upbuilding and Awakening*.[1]

---

[1] Princeton University Press, 1983.

Holden, nevertheless, could certainly benefit from an upbuilding of morale, and his unsettled state of mind seems to have resulted precisely from his jarring adolescent awakening to the unpleasant realities of the world. Kierkegaard takes his point of departure for a philosophical study of the concept of despair from the contrary New Testament passage in the Gospel of John 4:11: "This sickness is not unto death." As Holden fixes pathologically on the misery and disappointment of all that is hideous and physically nauseating in his surroundings, his outlook appears to be something less drastic, approximating only a sickness unto barfing, or at least a violent dry retching.

Fear and Loathing at Pencey

The word "disgust" does not actually occur anywhere in Salinger's story, although the word "disgusting" appears exactly once. We find Holden resorting to this terminology near the novel's beginning to describe his parting visit with his history teacher Spencer, just before leaving the Pencey School with his Gladstone bags and sporting his impulsively purchased red peaked hunting cap. Holden writes in his memoir about the significant incidents leading up to his nervous breakdown and institutionalization, recalling an encounter that understandably filled him with visceral disgust:

> Old Spencer started nodding again. He also started picking his nose. He made out like he was only pinching it, but he was really getting the old thumb right in there. I guess he thought it was all right to do because it was only me that was in the room. I didn't care, except that it's pretty disgusting to watch somebody pick their nose. (2, pp. 13–14)

Body functions and their biological byproducts are especially offensive to Holden. He endures a one-sided interview with Spencer, in which his history teacher eviscerates the student's laughably incompetent final essay on the ancient Egyptians. Holden remarks that Spencer handles this "like it was a turd or something" (2, p. 15). He offers this pencil sketch:

> The minute I went in, I was sort of sorry I'd come. He was reading the *Atlantic Monthly*, and there were pills and medicine all over the

place, and everything smelled like Vicks Nose Drops. It was pretty depressing. I'm not too crazy about sick people, anyway. What made it even more depressing, old Spencer had on this very sad, ratty old bathrobe that he was probably born in or something. I don't much like to see old guys in their pajamas and bathrobes anyway. Their bumpy old chests are always showing. And their legs. Old guys' legs, at beaches and places, always look so white and unhairy. (2, p. 11)

Nor is Spencer the exclusive subject of Holden's feelings of revulsion. Salinger unforgettably portrays another even more annoying person in Holden's orbit at the Pencey School, as oblivious to his own disgusting appearance and behavior as to his unwanted social presence. The pathetically awkward Robert Ackley is indelibly recounted by Holden in his final hours as he prepares to make tracks in disgrace once again from the academy he has recently entered and even more recently come to deplore.

The very sound of Ackley's name, repeated with just the right intonation, if we say it a couple of times, begins to sound rather like someone gagging on a rubbery piece of gristle, producing an onomatopoeic choking, which Salinger presumably intends. Perhaps as another reflection of Salinger's grim sense of humor, the young man's name is further phonetically redolent of the word "acne," which reportedly also fits Ackley's unfortunate dermatological condition. Holden introduces us to the wretched boy from the dorm room next door:

Even without looking up, I knew right away who it was. It was Robert Ackley, this guy that roomed right next to me. . . . He was a very peculiar guy. He was a senior, and he'd been at Pencey the whole four years and all, but nobody ever called him anything except "Ackley." Not even Herb Gale, his own roommate, ever called him "Bob" or even "Ack." If he ever gets married, his own wife'll probably call him "Ackley." . . . The whole time he roomed next to me, I never even once saw him brush his teeth. They always looked mossy and awful, and he damn near made you sick if you saw him in the dining room with his mouth full of mashed potatoes and peas or something. Besides that, he had a lot of pimples. Not just on his forehead or his chin, like most guys, but all over his whole face. And not only that, he had a terrible personality. (3, pp. 25–26)

It would be hard to cobble up a more compelling picture of disgusting human features all rolled together into a single contemptible dorm neighbor. Can we ever look complacently at or live in proximity to another human being again, once we have read this part of *The Catcher in the Rye*, without thinking of Holden's close scrutiny of Robert Ackley?

We must nevertheless appreciate the fact that Ackley is virtually Holden's only "friend" at Pencey, however dismal and dysfunctional their association. The firm foundation for their occasionally keeping company seems to be nothing more than the fact that Holden, unlike his fellow dorm mates, does not actually chase the boy away. Holden takes pity on the repulsive and otherwise socially ostracized and hopelessly clueless kid in this respect only, as he later tells his sister, the loyal Phoebe. He will not be mean to Ackley by excluding him from things as the other boys banished him from their phony self-important little school clubs and fraternities. Holden confides in his sister, as he tries to answer her question why he has thrown away another opportunity to make something of himself at yet another school:

> "Oh, God, Phoebe, don't ask me. I'm sick of everybody asking me that," I said. "A million reasons why. It was one of the worst schools I ever went to. It was full of phonies. And mean guys. You never saw so many mean guys in your life. For instance, if you were having a bull session in somebody's room, and somebody wanted to come in, nobody'd let them in if they were some dopey, pimply guy. Everybody was always locking their door when somebody wanted to come in. And they had this goddam secret fraternity that I was too yellow not to join. There was this one pimply, boring guy, Robert Ackley, that wanted to get in. He kept trying to join, and they wouldn't let him. Just because he was boring and pimply. I don't even feel like talking about it. It was a stinking school. Take my word." (22, pp. 217–18)

The disgusting images of seasoned history teacher Spencer digging his thumb in his nose, and Ackley with his mossy teeth masticating a messy mouthful of mashed potatoes, is already enough to make us sick, just as it viscerally makes the point that, whatever else is going on in Holden Caulfield's tortured psyche, he has rather strikingly fastened onto some of the most disgusting aspects of human biology and social behavior.

Holden is not psychologically prepared to overlook the disgusting, as most of us must do every day in order to get along with the business of life. Instead, the hyper-perceptive sixteen-year-old focuses on ordinary disgusting things with rapt attention, bordering on fascination, possibly as an excuse for withdrawing from participation in the social order he rejects. They call out to him, these dripping noses, skin diseases and slobbering mouths, and he gives them his full consideration, almost as if to savor what he finds disgusting, especially in the people immediately around him.

"Hell is—other people", concludes philosopher Jean-Paul Sartre in his 1944 one-act play, *Huis Clos (No Exit)*, written about the same time that Salinger was composing the short stories for magazines that were eventually incorporated into *The Catcher in the Rye*.[2] Holden, it seems, as the novel progresses, would wholeheartedly agree. He is filled with disgust at the personal habits of almost everyone with whom he is obliged to interact. A student cutting his fingernails onto the floor, his own roommate doing one better by publicly cutting his toenails or popping his pimples, alcoholics, cheaters, liars, the snot and urine that befoul the urban landscape, the elderly with their unpleasant physical infirmities, the flits, jerks, fakes and phonies with whom Holden feels besieged. There is even a token fleabag hotel transvestite thrown in for good measure. The seemingly endless parade of nauseating encounters is punctuated only by the rare act of generosity, understanding, or moral or aesthetic unpretentiousness, that Holden likes to say just kills him or knocks him out.

We're naturally led to ask what it could mean for Holden to be so sensitive to what is disgusting. Why does he attach so much importance to these human foibles, as he recounts the recent events of his journey from another scorched-earth school term to the dreaded confrontation with his parents at their apartment in New York City? The novel, presented entirely in Holden's own voice, is imaginably recorded in the notebook a psychiatrist might have asked him to keep for diagnostic and therapeutic reasons. From its pages we discover only in the final brief chapter that for the moment at least Holden has ended up in some kind of clinic or hospital. There the narrative

---

[2] *No Exit and Three Other Plays*, Vintage, 1946, p. 47.

abruptly ends, in the institution where Holden, having suffered a breakdown and trying to understand what has happened to him, is presumably under professional observation.

There is, accordingly, a psychological story to be told about Salinger's memorable character, the emotionally inwardly disturbed Holden Caulfield. Moreover, there is a captivating conceptual dimension to Holden's alienation from his fellow human beings that we can approach by considering what one philosopher who has investigated the subject with some care has had to say about feelings of disgust and the disgusting.

Kolnai's Phenomenology of Disgust

What is disgust? What does it mean for Holden to be disgusted? Holden finds old Spencer's nostril spelunking disgusting, Salinger is clear. But what can *philosophy* offer to help us understand Holden's state of mind as Salinger unwraps Holden's story? We can explore the concept of disgust philosophically by considering Aurel Kolnai's brilliant 1927 phenomenological study, *Disgust (Der Ekel).*[3]

Kolnai is certainly not the first thinker to have remarked on the philosophical peculiarities of disgust. Plato in his dialogue, *Parmenides* 130b1–e5, presents a dramatic interaction between a youthful Socrates and the elder Presocratic statesman of metaphysics, Parmenides. The old man in his greater wisdom challenges the Platonic theory that there are ideal eternal abstract *Forms* or *Ideas* of such noble properties as virtue, beauty, justice, and love, by questioning whether there must not also exist Forms for "disgusting" or "vile" things, such as "nail, hair, and dirt." Similarly, in the *Phaedrus*, Socrates, much like Holden, contrasts the beauty of a youthful lover with the indignity and disgusting appearance of the same person at an imagined advanced age.

Since not even Socrates can make up his mind as to whether there are abstract Forms of disgusting things, we had better look for a philosophical explanation of the phenomenon a bit closer to home.[4]

---

[3] Aurel Kolnai, *On Disgust*, Open Court, 2004.

[4] Plato, *Phaedrus* 240d8–e5: "The beloved must look at a face that is old and past its prime, and other things that go along with that which it is

Exceptions aside, and they are rare indeed, it is fair to say that philosophers for the most part have not devoted concentrated attention to the topic that we find in Kolnai. Kolnai was a Hungarian philosophy student at the University of Vienna, Austria, in the early part of the twentieth century. He studied with a number of the most famous thinkers of the day, and eventually became an enthusiastic follower of the intentionalist empirical philosophy of psychology developed by Franz Brentano, and of Brentano's student Edmund Husserl's phenomenology.

Phenomenology is a school of philosophy that practices a kind of descriptive philosophical psychology, in which the structural features of thought are systematically isolated from others and categorized according to their distinctive features discernible by a disciplined introspection or internal perception (*innere Wahrnehmung*). Classical phenomenology distinguishes between a *mental act*, its accompanying *content*, and *intended object*, or what the thought is *about*.

Kolnai's investigations of the feeling of disgust are a contribution to the phenomenology of disgust as a very particular emotion (Kolnai, pp. 30–33). Kolnai methodically divides the "delimitation" of disgust by invoking a number of characteristic phenomenologically distinguishable "points of view." In this way, he identifies the essential content and intentions of disgust, which he systematizes into a phenomenological theory. He describes his purpose and advocates the need for a phenomenology of disgust in these terms:

> The problem of disgust has to my knowledge been thus far sorely neglected. In comparison to the scientific (psychological and metaphysical) interest that has been applied to hatred and fear [*Angst*], not to mention aversion or displeasure [*Unlust*], disgust—although a common and important element of our emotional life—is a hith-

---

unpleasant even to hear talked about, let alone to deal with when one is constantly compelled to confront them: being suspiciously guarded all the time against everybody; and hearing . . . criticisms that are intolerable when he is sober but when he is in his cups and indulges freely in coarse and uninhibited language, become not only intolerable but disgusting" (*The Symposium and the Phaedrus: Plato's Erotic Dialogues*, State University of New York Press, 1993).

erto unexplored sphere. . . . But considered for itself the feeling or attitude of disgust possesses a unique and characteristic quality, which is at one and the same time difficult to clarify and not something which can be taken as a primitive phenomenon of the natural world (like, say, attraction and repulsion). Thus a phenomenological investigation seems here to be highly appropriate. (*On Disgust*, p. 29)

We can think of Salinger's novel as providing the raw material for a phenomenological investigation of the nature of disgust like Kolnai's. We have the unique first-person account of Holden's feelings as he later recalls them in a running stream-of-consciousness commentary that carries us along from episode to episode. Holden undergoes a highly personalized version of despair and Kierkegaardian sickness unto death at the appalling aspects of humanity that, to the best of our abilities, we ordinarily prefer to ignore. We're permitted to eavesdrop on Holden's thoughts in the notebook he has prepared, the novel itself as we have it from Salinger's pen.

The forthright phenomenological voyeurism we are granted of Holden Caulfield's thoughts indicates from his own inside perspective that he is not fashionably posing as a young man sick of life. He is the genuine article, and he is genuinely ill. But of what? What is his malady, and how and why has it come about? He mentions flatly in the final chapter, and almost as an aside, after he returns to New York to the bosom of his family, "I got sick and all"; while in the very next paragraph, he mentions obliquely "this one psychoanalyst guy they have here" (26, p. 276). What do we learn about Holden's experience of disgust from Kolnai's phenomenological analysis, and how can we combine it with Salinger's fictional phenomenology of Holden's state of mind, in order to understand what the woeful teenager is going through?

Kolnai explains the relation between sense experience and disgust, when he maintains:

The main carriers of the sensation of disgust are the olfactory, visual, and tactile senses. . . . Here already attention may be drawn to the interconnections between disgust, smell, putrescence, decay, secretion, life, nourishment. Here we have a range of interconnections among intentions of various kinds which is entirely lacking in the case of fear, and which also in the case of hate does not exist in such a naturalistically definable form. (*On Disgust*, pp. 48–50)

Previously, Kolnai had remarked: "Hate and even anger are less bound up with bodily phenomena than is disgust, in spite of the more violent physical phenomena attendant upon anger. This is because the sensuous impressions involved in disgust and the suggestion of a physical reaction of vomiting play here a more essential role in a way that is more concrete than the raging, kicking, and throwing which may arise through anger" (p. 32).

Kolnai's comparison of disgust with fear and hate is crucial to his philosophical interpretation, and not merely because these emotions are sometimes superficially confused and mistaken for disgust. We may fear the dark, but we are seldom if ever disgusted by it, and it is by such associations and discriminating association failures that Kolnai pieces together his phenomenological inquiry into what is distinctive about the disgusting.

What's crucial in Kolnai's phenomenology of disgust and the disgusting fits Holden's case rather exactly. Kolnai concludes that disgust is one of several aversion mechanisms by which we turn away from potential sources of danger or distress. Like hate and fear, but with a unique phenomenological character of its own, disgust serves as a signal to avoid something that we might find harmful. We can appreciate Kolnai's point concretely when we consider that rotting substances, vehicles of disease and corruption, are among the kinds of things we stereotypically find disgusting. Feeling disgusted at them helps to alert us to their undesirable and often hazardous presence, as a natural psychological instrument contributing to our survival, health and happiness.

We can describe Holden's disgust in just this way, provided we understand both the intended object of his disgust and the reason why he might need to defend his fragile emotional condition by means of aversion-supporting reaction. Although Kolnai emphasizes the olfactory centricity of disgust, what seems to trigger disgust for Holden is more often visual. Salinger represents Holden's waves of disgust as episodes of Holden's being "depressed," or, more vividly in his slang-ridden vocabulary, "depressed as hell." From Kolnai's phenomenological standpoint, Salinger hits the nail directly on the head in relating Holden's feelings of disgust by any other name to body functions in particular and their sometimes horrid byproducts, exemplified for Holden, almost as though by a Platonic archetype, in the ungainly person of Robert Ackley.

There's something more to the nature of disgust, according to Kolnai. He discovers that when disgust is occasioned by auditory stimulus it is generally accompanied by a moral judgment:

> When I find a seductive melody disgusting then the sensation I experience is vividly of the moral disgustingness of drunkenness, of unclean breath, and so forth; the sound of chewing and lip-smacking conjures up an optical portrait of greed and gluttony. . . . One would search in vain for any even approximately equivalent parallel in the aural sphere to something like a putrid smell, the feel of a flabby body, or of a belly ripped open. (*On Disgust*, p. 49)

There is a moral dimension of at least some categories of disgust that makes it phenomenologically different also from fear and hate and related aversion reactions. As a prelude to this set of remarks, Kolnai declares: "All aural disgust is to a considerable extent 'moral disgust'; it presupposes a sufficiency of associations called forth in succession by the objects which in visual disgust are consigned to a far greater extent to the background of the intention" (p. 49).

This is reflected also in Holden's incidents of disgust, a parallel linkage of physical response especially to visual rather than auditory cues, and a moral reaction to what Holden finds objectionable about the world. All that remains now is to connect the dots and we shall have a nearly complete picture of the inescapable feelings of disgust that are defeating Holden and beating him down into a sorry state of dejection, lethargy, despondency and indirection, as the anti-hero of Salinger's timeless American coming-of-age novel.

Holden's Self-Administered Aversion Therapy

If Kolnai is right that disgust is an aversive defense reaction, then what, according to Salinger, does a disgusted Holden Caulfield have to defend himself against?

We can speculate from the first twenty-five chapters of Salinger's novel that Holden finally breaks down psychologically as his sense of disgust crescendos, that he has been overwhelmed by something in his life. We learn eventually, reading between Salinger's lines, that Holden is recovering all too slowly from the death of his younger brother Allie. Part of the novel's abiding charm is that it so realistically raises questions about a young person dealing with the fact of a death in the family. Salinger offers the foundation throughout the work for a number of different realistic interpretations of Holden's character, his decisions and actions, as Salinger spins the adventure, and as the cause, finally, of his being at least temporarily institutionalized. We might propose, in this vein, without meaning to exclude other interesting interpretations, that the main driving force of Holden's character in Salinger's fiction is the persistent survivor guilt Holden suffers over the loss of Allie to leukemia.

One of Holden's dramatic neurotic symptoms as he lurches toward the book's denouement is his increasingly heightened sense of the absurdity and brute injustice of the world. It must be a cold unsympathetic universe that could snuff out the life of such a wonderful brother as Allie, two years Holden's junior, who never got angry, and always had such smart and thoughtful things to say. Who else but Allie would write poems in green ink on his baseball glove to occupy downtime moments in the outfield? It is the loss of Allie that has plummeted Holden into a relentless overpowering textbook depressive funk.

Holden is defeated by a feeling of futility in anything he might otherwise try to do. He sees no good enough reason to direct his energies in any direction, except, as we know from his midnight talk with Phoebe, to be the catcher in a field of rye who rescues children dancing and playing in the grain before they can tumble to their doom over the edge of an abyss. Holden would save those children, innocents like Phoebe, if only he could, where he was powerless to save Allie.

Holden's depression seems to be the result of his debilitating psychologically irrepressible obsessive reflections on Allie's death and the nature of existence and the human condition, the meaninglessness of life in a purposeless, indifferent and unyielding universe. Holden has gone through extraordinarily emotionally trying times since Allie's untimely death. He dwells morbidly on an incident he continues to regret, in which he had forbidden Allie to accompany him and a neighborhood friend Bobby Fallon to Lake Sedebego for the day on their bikes to shoot their BB guns (14, p. 129). In time, we learn that Holden continues to talk out loud as though to his deceased brother, especially when he is under stress.

While it seems to Holden that other persons around him—personified in bold relief this time by his despised roommate, the manifest future statesman or corporate CEO Stradlater—are stupidly insensitive to what Holden sees so clearly, Holden can only wish himself away from one school to another, and from everything there that he finds exceedingly repulsive. Stradlater, despite his athleticism, handsome good looks and enviable if exaggeratedly reported success with girls, is, in a completely different way, even more disgusting to Holden than Ackley.

Holden's bully roommate resorts to physical assault when Holden tears up the composition Stradlater had first buddy-commissioned him to write on "Anything descriptive. . . . Just as long as it's descriptive as hell" (4, p. 37), and then rejects when Holden writes about his brother's baseball glove as not meeting the assignment requirements. Now we can feel Holden's disgust at the other persons with whom he must keep company at the Pencey School. The petty annoyances of daily existence there are simply too much for Holden to bear as he tries to cope with the loss of Allie geographically far away from the other Allie-surviving members of his grief-ridden family. He's overcome with rage especially when he thinks of how he would rather still be with Allie, a thing he knows to be impossible, or with Phoebe, when he is being only somewhat more sensible and down to earth.

It's for much the same reason that Holden is disgusted with his history teacher Spencer. The moral dimension that Kolnai emphasizes in his phenomenology of auditorily induced disgust is precisely what is loathsome to Holden. Holden despises old people because, unlike Allie, they have had the hostile universe's fickle luck to survive to a ripe age, while his splendid brother was snatched away from him for no good reason and, to use a simple-minded school-yard expression, with no possibility of do-overs.

If Kolnai is right in his central thesis about the phenomenology of disgust as an aversion defense reaction, then it's relatively easy to imagine how Holden's disgust works to protect him. Holden defends himself against further unbearable disappointment and misery by exaggerating the sense of disgust with which we are mostly thankfully affected only to a much more limited extent. He is thereby shielded from the kind of pain and sorrow he has experienced over the death of Allie by being so disgusted with the reminders and potential sources of despair surrounding him every day that he flees from them, as he does symbolically from yet another detested prep school.

If he is disgusted by Pencey, and believes everyone there is unworthy of his time and company, then he does not have to try to succeed. There is no good reason in that case to invest the slightest energy in working toward the kind of career that he thinks he sees through as the meaningless empty victory of bogus fakes, frauds, posers and social counterfeits, although at another level in his confused thinking he recognizes that he should. He just *can't*.

Holden is protected by his own sense of the world's meaninglessness, the futility of trying to do anything worthwhile in a universe where Allie could be so cruelly and senselessly eliminated. His profound sense of disgust repels him from anything that might later disappoint him, because he simply cannot deal with more disappointment in his life. His disgust keeps him removed from things, and prevents him from involvement with people and purposes that might eventually cause him more emotional pain than he could bear, beyond what he is already suffering over Allie's death. If old people disgust him, so do the girls he knows, the prostitute Sunny with whom he cannot bring himself to consummate a negotiated liaison, the abrasive words "Fuck you" scrawled on the wall where his precious sister Phoebe must pass on her way to school, and many other things besides.

The repulsive people that surround Holden are squandering life's opportunities with their stupidities, opportunities that should have much more deservedly belonged to Allie. They dare to exist where Allie should be instead, inhabiting the beautiful world that could have existed if only Allie hadn't absurdly died, a world that Holden, especially in his disingenuous suicidal moments in the novel, thinks of himself in comparison also as unworthy to enjoy.

If anything is going to heal Holden from his sickness of heart, it can only be the passage of time and the insuperable bright promise for the future represented by the Allie-like goodness of his younger sister Phoebe. Holden grasps this distant possibility intuitively and ineffably, gravitating naturally toward the girl as his last hope, which he may someday come to realize more self-consciously as offering himself and the miserable world at large another chance.[5]

---

[5] For related interpretations with a distinctively different emphasis, see especially the essays by Arthur Mizener, Alfred Kazin, and John Updike in *Salinger: The Classic Critical and Personal Portrait*, edited by Henry Anatole Grunwald (Harper Brothers, 1962), and the more recent collection, *If You Really Want to Hear about It: Writers on J.D. Salinger and His Work*, edited by Catherine Crawford (Thunder's Mouth, 2006).

11
Being and Phoniness

RUSSELL MANNING

When Holden says "people are always ruining things for you," this is not just the rant of a disaffected youth (12, p. 114). It's an accurate assessment of certain parts of our world.

Catcher in the Rye is often interpreted as a novel about a deteriorating mind, the downward spiral of teen existential angst, or even a young man's decline into alienation. I disagree. I think it's a travelogue of the world that he encounters. That's also our world. That's our phoniness and it makes the novel as much about us as about him.

Most of the time when we stop to think and look around we quickly come to the conclusion that things can get pretty crappy. The crap and the phonies are not just a matter of perspective. There are *real* crappy and phony people and objects all over the place. Stop and take a look at where you are now. The air conditioner might be on the blink, the television is showing repeats (or worse, shows that should never be repeated), the news is full of tragedy and stupidity (and that's just the reporters and presenters), and you haven't got enough money to buy what the you-know-who-corporation is trying to sell you.

Most of us would shrug and go on suffering the heat or the cold, watching the television or eyeing with envy the guy next door with the latest gadget. Life can be crap, full of phonies and morons, unattainable sexual partners, bad food and acne. But this doesn't mean we alone are loopy. There are things awry with the culture in which we live.

Chimps Wearing Pants Riding Bikes

By treating Holden as not just a victim but as an interpreter of crap and phonies we may move closer to an understanding of where crap and phoniness come from.

Our first philosophical "move" is to stop and think why our lives are the way they are; to examine the everyday stuff in our heads, the people we encounter as well as the everyday objects in life and what they *really* have to do with everyday existing. Philosophers call this *phenomenology*, the study of how consciousness appears to the individual. But we must be careful here. We are not just talking about how we see and interpret the world, but how the world "comes" to minds, how consciousness is structured from a first-person direct account.

When we think phenomenologically we pay attention to how our mood affects reality and for Holden mood is a significant factor in how he meets and then interprets the world. According to a twentieth- century philosopher who was a pioneer in phenomenology, Martin Heidegger (1889–1976), we have to judiciously take apart the everyday and look for how we respond to it. This he would call the "authenticity" in it, where external meanings are minimized in favor of a first-person account. *The Catcher in the Rye* recounts Holden's search for an authenticity, a search which nearly drives him nuts.

So when Holden tells us about newsreels and says "Christ almighty. There's always a dumb horse race, and some dame breaking a bottle over a ship, and some chimpanzee riding a goddam bicycle with pants on" (17, p. 173), we can say in phenomenological terms that Holden is more than just infuriated by the newsreels. Horse races, ship dedications, and monkey cyclists create a specific "attitude" for him that we can investigate. We shouldn't just jump to the conclusion that the problem is with Holden's response. We should also investigate the culture that encourages apes to be filmed riding bikes!

We can challenge those people who think that primates on bikes are "cute" and demand that they justify how they see the world as normal or natural. They would say that is just the way the world is, with bike-riding monkeys, dames breaking bottles on ships, and horse races. But are encounters like these natural or normal, and as such should they just be accepted? Not for Holden. Holden is deeply concerned about everyday things in his life. Let's get more technical and talk about his "being." Holden tries—but ultimately fails—to understand fully his *being* by paying attention to the people and objects he encounters. In summary, he does phenomenology.

However, we rarely focus our attention on the everyday. As Heidegger would say, the everyday recedes or withdraws into the background. Look where you are now, the desk you are sitting at, the person sitting next to you on the bus, the bookstore you're in (go ahead and buy the book you cheapskate!). These are everyday events and until I mentioned them they were probably hidden in the background of your awareness because chances are you were not "tuned" into them. Now they're revealed as if they have emerged into your mind, revealed by your being as it encounters them. Holden spends his days in the novel making the everyday emerge for himself and his readers. He pays attention to them, his attitude is reflected in them and we get privileged access to his world by following his attitude to the everyday encounters he has.

Getting Sexy with the Everyday

Holden's phenomenological insights include this:

> I hate fist fights. I don't mind getting hit so much—although I'm not crazy about it naturally—but what scares me the most in a fist fight is the guy's face. I can't stand looking at the other guy's face, is my trouble. It wouldn't be so bad if you both could be blindfolded or something. It's a funny kind of yellowness, when you come to think of it, but its yellowness all right. I'm not kidding myself. (13, p. 117)

Here Holden doesn't just tell us that he's a chicken but what it feels like to be a chicken. By interrogating his chicken-ness Holden exposes how the everyday is so ingrained into our psyche that we take it far too much for granted. Holden tunes into the everyday so we can see how this everyday has such a grip on us.

Sometimes he's tuned in just a little too close. When he gets too close to tuning in about Ackley's acne or Luce's sex life we get a glimpse of how important the everyday is to him and, upon reflection, how it is to us. We see this when he tells old Luce:

"You know what the trouble with me is? I can never get really sexy—
I mean *really* sexy—with a girl I don't like a lot. I mean I have to like
her a lot. If I don't, I sort of lose my goddam desire for her and all. Boy,
it really screws up my sex life something awful. My sex life stinks." (19,
p.191)

When we meet Holden he is "thrown" into the everyday. These
small everyday reflections show just how involved and important the everyday becomes. Most of our life is immersed in the
everyday. What makes Holden special is that because life buf-
fets him around and he tries hard to stop the phoniness from
getting him down, he spends an inordinate amount of time
coming to terms with his moods, brought about in part by his
everyday surroundings.

He spends his day trying to separate the average from the
special, the everyday from the unique, and the superficial from
the deep. He worries about people, his (lack of) sex life, suicide,
smoking, religion, movies, the Museum of Natural History, and
the list goes on. For Holden, life is an anxious yearning. There's
nothing unusual about that, because we all can be anxious and
we all can yearn. He is, we could say, attempting to gain something more authentic, a philosophical search if there ever was
one.

Before we're conscious of things in the world like the desk,
the person, or the bookstore, they are concealed, because we do
not pay attention to them or care about them. We have to call
them to our attention, to bring them into focus so they become
part of our being in the world. They reveal themselves when
you bring them into your being's focus. Otherwise they with-
draw again and conceal themselves and the world works
smoothly.

Everyday Being-in-the-World at Pencey

From the very opening sentence of the novel Holden Caulfield
is a square peg in a round hole. According to Heidegger we
shouldn't ask why we're square, but who made the round hole
without telling us. Holden doesn't see himself fitting comfort-
ably in the world of Pencey or New York or his family's home.
He doesn't even really fit inside his own skin. His feeling can
be explained by working through Holden's unusual relation-

ship with himself. He rarely stops to examine the problematic relationship he has being in his own skin. But this is something we're constantly drawn to and through fly-on-the-wall observation of Holden's environment, we see his world as dysfunctional, not just Holden himself. When Holden declares that the world and every sunuvabitch in it irritates him we might even be able to argue that he must include himself in this assessment because of this lack of total self-assessment.

We might demand that Holden ask himself why he always shifts the blame of the crappy, boring, phoney world as a problem with the world. Perhaps it might be an alarm bell going off to tell him something fundamentally important about himself and how our basic attitude affects our being-in-the-world. Here Heidegger has some interesting things to say.

Holden's attitude to the world gives a clue to being. We can go back to the notion of square pegs in round holes. Being is often feeling like a square peg in a square hole, where living is reasonably smooth, predictable and functional. It's like riding a bike; it's only when we hit a bump that we notice that things are not really that smooth. We call our being into question. As you read this sentence, it's not until you stop to think that you are being by sitting there reading that your being is "called into question." Heidegger says we must pay as much attention to the being that is sitting there, being there, as the physical body that is there.

The next thing we notice is that being is always about moods. Riding a bike is exciting, potholes and bumps are not; they are often dangerous and thus mood changing. Holden is always in a mood that colors and textures his attitude to his being. In every interaction in the book, from first to last, Holden's mood is governed by his response to those with whom he engages. Their exchanges reflect something very important to Heidegger. They are everyday occurrences but they tell us something very important about being.

When he is being Holden, his everyday worries about his exchanges with others in the world defines who he is. When we think this through in our own cases, we realize that we're not independent self-contained autonomous selves. Being is "dealing with," and as such is a process and not a thing. Holden is not just a sixteen-year-old student at Pencey. He is what that sixteen-year-old does and feels while he is doing his everyday tasks at Pencey. This was crucial for Heidegger. Being is doing, not a thing, but a thing doing.

When we first meet Holden he has been expelled from the expensive Pencey Prep for recurrent poor grades. He gives us an account of the school and the people that he mixes with in it. His everyday observations are understandably jaundiced. Holden thinks that the claims that Pencey makes about being a "good school" molding "fine characters" is "strictly for the birds." There are only two good people at Pencey, most are "crooks," "phonies," or just aggravations. What the reader is struck most by in these opening pages is Holden's mood. A real square peg in a round hole.

For Heidegger the way that we live, or to be more precise in Heidegger's language, the way we are being in the world, is always encountered through mood. We are always "in a mood" and when you think this through he is stating something uncontroversial. We are anxious, frightened, upset, calm or bored. We encounter day to day experience in moods of varying and contingent degrees. But here the important terms is "in." We are *in* the mood in the world. We cannot escape either world or mood, and a moment of phenomenological reflection will tell us that our mood is always part of the fact of being-in-the-world.

More importantly we care, or we should care deeply about the moods that we carry with us and how they relate to, and shape and influence our experiences. For Heidegger caring about moods was to care about the mine-ness of moods. Mine-ness is a Heideggerian way of saying what belongs to my way of being. What part of existence belongs to and is experienced by me. Existing this way is being-in-the-world; it is special and unique to *Homo sapiens* because we are the only species to reflect self consciously on their mine-ness. Yet this is always experienced as average every day activity as every moment in time we are being with respect to our mine-ness.

However, we experience this already being there, not joined to the world but as we have said, being a vital component in it. The world is an inexhaustible network of things, of which we are just one. Mood brings these things into view. We are not outsiders struggling to understand the world, but rather we are inside our own experience with the world interpreted by our own capacity to interpret, reflect and respond to it. For

Heidegger, mood was always present and we can only make one mood by way of another. This is the only way we can be. When we're absorbed in the world rather than absorbed with ourselves we're not acting with enough attention to ourselves, we are being in Heidegger's term "inauthentic."

Ackley and the Inauthentic

What choice did you have to read this book? What choice did you have to become fascinated with *The Catcher in the Rye*? One of the great puzzles that have always perplexed philosophers is freedom. When we make a decision, to what extent can we say that this decision is truly ours? When we think and talk about our own lifestyle, exactly how much have we chosen for ourselves and how much is the result of contingent factors that are not truly and totally ours?

Holden's encounters with characters throughout the novel are prime examples of what Heidegger meant by being authentic and inauthentic. Remember Heidegger took a different view of being in the world and his definition of authentic is not what we would immediately think. For Heidegger freedom and authenticity was the ability to be able to be in the most control possible at our deepest level of being. He doesn't quite mean real. He means avoiding the inauthentic (phoniness) of what is the current trend or fashion. But here we can learn from Holden.

Take for example Holden's attitude to reading. He loves books (even though he tells us he is illiterate) and his judgment of what might be a good book is based on whether he would like the author to be his friend after he has finished reading the book. We see here Holden coming close to talking about his essential feelings, the structure of his basic everyday mood revealed to us through his relationships with reading fiction. This unique way of judging his reading has nothing to do with the status of the author or more importantly what others in his life say about them, how well the books sell or what awards they might win. Instead we get to see how Holden comes to them, how they reveal or disclose to Holden his innermost moods. Here a book that "kills" him or "knocks him out" is an authentic assessment of his mood because he is declaring through these violent words (kill and knock out) how his being is disturbed by what he has read, as if he has been fighting with it.

For Heidegger, feeling this way tells us what we feel about ourselves, not how the world makes us feel. This way of thinking about our feelings comes before we name them. We feel good about reading something, then we start to examine why we feel good. Holden likes Ring Lardner as he reads him *then* he tries to work out why he likes him and he relies on his innermost feelings, his own emotional compass to guide him.

This is authentic feeling in Heidegger's terms. Holden doesn't read Ring Lardner because Ackley or Stradlater or old Spencer does. Holden's reading choices are more authentic because he chooses them without relating his choice to what others are doing, thinking or saying. They can never be completely free choices because Holden lives in a certain place at a certain time where social choices are to a certain extent shaped by the market and the economic and political circumstances, but his are more authentic.

Ackley is in many ways inauthentic because his actions are always premised on the reactions of others, what others will think of him. He is nasty, jealous and has questionable teeth. Similarly Holden's confrontation with Sally Hayes demonstrates inauthenticity. Sally says:

> "Oh darling, I love you too," she said. Then right in the same damn breath, she said, "Promise me you'll let your hair grow. Crew cuts are getting corny. And your hair's so lovely." (17, p. 163)

We see that Holden has a point. Inauthentic beings can radically alter moods. Like a burst pimple perhaps we need to avoid them. They are out there. Heidegger was fascinated with this word the "they."

New York Man (Das Man)

Holden encounters antagonism all throughout the novel. One of the interesting questions that we can ask is why some of the people he encounters produce so much anxiety in him. A refreshing way to think of this is as a problem with the world and not with Holden. Recall his remark about the guy with the strong handshake: "He was one of the guys that that think they're being a pansy if they don't break forty or fifty of your fingers when they shake hands with you. God I hate that stuff" (12, p. 113).

Heidegger offers us a really interesting take on such phonies. Nobody should be surprised by his action because we have come to expect such displays of machismo from their types. Heidegger is not critical of this machismo but the process which makes it appear natural, so that only Holden is tuned in to seeing it as something strange and out of the ordinary. When he does this and brings our attention to it we may be jolted out of this unexamined way of seeing the world and see a clearer version of the whole activity.

Heidegger thinks common attitudes and displays (like breaking guys' fingers in a handshake) are acted out because of a certain way the world is, a pre-given attitude that men are taught to be by the society they are in. Holden sees that the character he names Blop stands there like a guy with a poker up his ass, and we can see what he means. Navy guys are taught to stand there with pokers up their assess and break your hands when they shake it. They are taught to do it. Who teaches them? "They" do.

For Heidegger "they" comes about because of the network of acceptable social forces that license behavior. So men can know how to act manly by squeezing hard when shaking hands, or visiting prostitutes, or going to the movies all the time. They do it because it's acceptable and traditional. As such it fades into the background.

Have a look around you now, and if you don't tune in to what people are doing, life seems normal and reasonable. But much of what is going on around you is mass behavior domesticated by a form of an "authority of the they." This "they" makes so much of our everyday activity seem normal and acceptable, but it is only when we have our attention drawn to it that it can seem unusual or even strange. Holden finds this strange or abnormal behaviour around every corner, in every movie theatre or in every bar.

But it leads us into trouble when we stop to really think about the origins of such behavior. This is exactly what Holden does. He's full of anxiety in the presence of the Blop, or Sunny the prostitute, or Stadlater, because in part all these characters are like the "they." Mass activity such as watching films and listening to music can be inauthentic because we just follow the crowd absorbed into the world of the "they" without any real discrimination.

Getting Set to Puke

We've talked about Holden's moods and how they are always tuned in to the phony and the crappy. Sometimes he infuriates us by being phony and crappy himself, but most times he admits it. This is because there's no possibility to be completely authentic and self-creative. Holden drinks too much and smokes too much in the three days we spend with him, but there's enough evidence for us to argue that because of his anxiety at being-in-the-world he does do some things which we could claim as authentic. It's easy to spot the phony behavior and the book is top heavy with them, for example, Ackley's religious devotion, Stradlater's attitude to women, and so on.

In the end we have to come down on Holden's side. I say this, because many commentators on the book seem to be convinced that Holden's "taking it easy" confirms that he has suffered some form of paralyzing breakdown. The commentator's world itself is the one that we should feel comfortable with. They argue Holden is broken and a spell in the real world will fix him. But does this argument really hold up when we examine it?

Holden is extremely critical of a social system that is premised on superficial images, and this disturbs him enough to make him rebel. He's anxious about his place in the world not just because of the way *he* feels but because of the way that the world *is*. Things are not right for him and they may be not right for us. Here an authentic response is to examine our place in the world, how our being-in-the-world is at our mercy or at the mercy of the attitudes of those around us. That should make us feel anxious, but that might be a good thing because it will also challenge us to question the way that the phonies attempt to control the behavior of the rest.

In the end a phenomenological reading of *Catcher in the Rye* offers us much to say about being in the world. Authentic behavior according to Heidegger is that which emanates from the being which is ours, not dominated by the "they." Don't let commentaries convince you that Holden is merely a victim of teen existential angst. Sometimes the biggest phonies are the ones who write books telling you how to think (Dammit!)[1]

---

[1] For more on Heidegger's phenomenology I highly recommend *Heidegger Explained* by Graham Harman, Open Court, 2007.

12
Holden and Other Lunatics

JAN WHITT

If you want to know the truth, the guy I like best in the Bible, next to Jesus, was that lunatic and all, that lived in the tombs and kept cutting himself with stones. I like him ten times as much as the Disciples, that poor bastard. (14, p. 130)

Holden Caulfield demands that we practice what we preach. One of the least socially engaged and most rebellious characters in American fiction, Holden criticizes passivity and the lack of human compassion in the world around him. Deeply aware of the importance of active engagement in social issues, Holden understands that too many people—including Christ's disciples and contemporary ministers in the Christian church—do not do what they demand of others.

Although some critics of *The Catcher in the Rye* characterize Holden as a lost, depressed soul who lacks a moral center and consider the novel inappropriate for adolescents, Holden's life actually provides an opportunity to discuss the importance of a principled and engaged life. Ironies and paradoxes essential to an understanding of the Bible are present in *The Catcher in the Rye*, and Holden's identification with the lunatic who roams among graves suggests lines by Emily Dickinson: "Much madness is divinest sense / To a discerning eye / Much sense the starkest madness" *(The Complete Poems of Emily Dickinson*, p. 435).

Like Dickinson, Holden understands the wisdom in what the world might consider lunacy. He admires the madman of biblical lore who rages among the tombstones and seeks salvation;

he scorns church hierarchies and the arrogance of Christian leaders who are uninvolved with those in need. By recognizing that "much madness is divinest sense," Holden sets himself apart and identifies with philosophers whose work is rooted in the history, principles, and values of Christianity.

Calling himself "sort of an atheist" (14, p. 130), Holden admittedly does not consider himself a Christian, but he respects Jesus and celebrates the selflessness of the nuns whom he observes. He understands that they commit their lives to a purpose that is too often considered insane; also, he understands that renouncing earthly wealth and caring for others are admired by many and emulated by few. Most importantly, he is sympathetic to those who actively engage in social issues.

The Catcher in the Rye is controversial, not only because it makes a hero out of a cynical young man, but also because it highlights difficult topics, such as the existence of God, the life of Christ, and the connection between admiring Christ and following his mandates. According to the Bible, Christianity depends upon compassion and human agency; however, those who actually follow Christ's teachings and exercise social responsibility are so revolutionary that they may be considered insane.

Although Holden Caulfield does not subscribe to a particular creed or religion, he abhors both phoniness and passivity. People whom he considers the most hypocritical are those who are the least likely to reach out to other human beings, including ministers and others ordinarily held in high esteem for their self-sacrifice. Holden admires Jesus, compliments the nuns who devote their lives to Christian principles, and suggests that God might in fact be intimately involved with the world He created.

Holden is unimpressed by those who fail to incorporate their Christian beliefs into their daily lives and who don't understand the revolutionary nature of their faith. Like Holden, Jesus admonished those who live halfheartedly and who risk little for those around them: "So, because you are lukewarm, and neither cold nor hot, I am about to spit you out of my mouth" (Revelation 3:16). With these words, the importance of passionate human engagement is clear.

In spite of his insights, Holden is stymied by his cynicism and despair: "I felt so lonesome, all of a sudden. I almost wished

I was dead" (7, p. 62); "I was sort of crying. I don't know why" (7, p. 68); "I almost wished I was dead" (13, p. 118); "What I really felt like, though, was committing suicide" (14, p. 136). Too often dismissed as adolescent angst, these statements indicate someone struggling with the reality he sees and unsure if he wants to exist in a world so at odds with his values. *The Catcher in the Rye* is a novel populated by those who are not committed to one another and not proactive in the world. Although Holden reveals them for who they are, he remains unable to move into a life of service.

Holden's Christian Philosophy

Modern Christian philosophy helps to illuminate Holden's character, and a study of Christian principles clarifies his belief that faith requires an active and visible commitment to the welfare of others. Holden's beliefs intersect often with those espoused by philosophers and theologians such as Dietrich Bonhoeffer, a German Lutheran pastor interested in Transcendental philosophy and its impact on Protestantism and Catholicism. In his writing—especially in *The Cost of Discipleship* (1937)—Bonhoeffer focuses on the teachings of Jesus and on Christ's command that his followers be socially responsible and live as instruments of justice.

Other Christian philosophers whose ideas are reflected in *The Catcher in the Rye* include Desiderius Erasmus, a Catholic priest, humanist, and theologian; Edmund Husserl, who was baptized into the Lutheran faith and is considered the founder of phenomenology; and Immanuel Kant, who believes in Christian morality but divorces himself from what he considers to be its superstitions and reliance upon church hierarchy.

Holden recognizes the investment of Jesus and the nuns in the lives of others and questions those whose faith is not visible; similarly, Erasmus, Husserl, and Kant are suspicious of a faith without tangible evidence, a perspective supported by Scripture:

> But someone will say, "You have faith and I have good deeds." Show me your faith apart from your deeds, and I by my deeds will show you my faith. . . . Do you want to be shown, you senseless person, that faith apart from deeds is dead? . . . You see that a person is justified

by deeds and not by faith alone. . . . For just as the body without the spirit is dead, so faith without deeds is also dead." (James 2:18, 20, 24, 26)

Other philosophers who argue for a connection between faith and deeds include Hans Küng, a Catholic priest and theologian who advocates for a system of global ethics; Paul Ricoeur, reared in a Protestant family, who contributes to discussions about phenomenology, moral philosophy, and hermeneutics and who calls for a philosophy of action; and Friedrich Schleiermacher, a German theologian and philosopher, who is considered the "Father of Modern Protestant Theology" and believes in working toward *summum bonum,* or the "highest good." Schleiermacher argues in *The Christian Faith* (1821–22) that religion is at the heart of action.

Other prominent figures also reinforce the themes in *The Catcher in the Rye.* They include Richard Swinburne, a Christian apologist who in *Faith and Reason* (1981) argues for the existence of God, and Paul Tillich, a Christian existentialist and German-American theologian. A Lutheran minister, Tillich wrote *Dynamics of Faith* (1957), in which he writes, "Faith is the state of being ultimately concerned" (p. 1).

One of the most ardent advocates of Christian principles is Sören Kierkegaard, a philosopher and theologian who focuses upon personal choice and the impact of one's behavior upon other people and upon the natural world. Known as an existentialist and humanist, Kierkegaard was schooled in literature, philosophy, psychology, and theology. In *Fear and Trembling* (1843), a treatise on love and faith; *Two Ages* (1846); and his journals, Kierkegaard deals with topics as varied as the existence of God and the way people compromise their individual selves in order to be part of the larger community or "public."

Like Kierkegaard, Holden is suspicious of social norms, the widely held perceptions about what constitutes appropriate behavior. In *The Catcher in the Rye,* only lunatics such as Jesus and the nuns live according to their own principles and ignore what others think of them.

Possibly best known for his belief in the "leap of faith," Kierkegaard argues that both romantic love and faith in God require a suspension of disbelief. Faith, he said, is not rooted in absolutes, and its very existence implies an awareness of its antithesis, doubt. Convinced about the importance of the individual and about Christian ethics as a way to live fully in the world, Kierkegaard argues for personal courage in the face of society's inevitable criticism, and his beliefs are reflected in Holden's concern for everything from Phoebe to the ducks in Central Park.

Holden's spontaneous response to those in need exemplifies what Kierkegaard would call "faith," and this faith coexists with Holden's skepticism about the existence of God. Holden's behavior matters more than any articulation of his faith, and his compassion sets him apart from others. By society's standards, he's a lunatic.

In *Papers and Journals*, Kierkegaard deals unflinchingly with the failure of those who espouse Christian beliefs but stop short of participating in revolutionary and righteous acts: "Now I ask: What does it mean that we continue to pretend everything is as it should be but call ourselves Christians on the basis of the New Testament, when the very thing that is the nerve of the New Testament, the in-and-for-itself, has disappeared from life?" (p. 544). Here, Kierkegaard suggests that even the Christians who have promised to live as Christ commanded have fallen short and have compromised the very essence of the New Testament message of self-sacrifice and commitment to others. If Christians do not actively emulate Jesus, Christianity is dead.

Holden's Struggle to Make Sense

In *The Catcher in the Rye,* an alienated Holden Caulfield struggles to find meaning in a universe that defies interpretation. Through stream of consciousness, J.D. Salinger allows Holden to move from essential issues to insignificant ones and back again. In the process, the protagonist explores the importance of the individual, the role of human responsibility, and a secular faith that is based on a suspension of reason and a belief in the absurd.

After Holden decides that he doesn't want to have sex with a prostitute, she leaves his hotel room and Holden tries to sleep. Agitated and lonely, he wants to pray but realizes he can't. The stream of consciousness that follows is one of the most poignant moments in the novel because Holden is forced

to confront his isolation and his identification with a madman
who wanders through a graveyard, tearing his clothing and
spouting gibberish:

> I can't always pray when I feel like it. In the first place, I'm sort of an
> atheist. I like Jesus and all, but I don't care too much for most of the
> other stuff in the Bible. Take the Disciples, for instance. They annoy
> the hell out of me, if you want to know the truth. They were all right
> after Jesus was dead and all, but while He was alive, they were about
> as much use to Him as a hole in the head. All they did was keep let-
> ting Him down. I like almost anybody in the Bible better than the
> Disciples. If you want to know the truth, the guy I like best in the Bible,
> next to Jesus, was that lunatic and all, that lived in the tombs and kept
> cutting himself with stones. I like him ten times as much as the
> Disciples, that poor bastard. (14, p. 130)

Holden's characterization (and dismissal) of the disciples of
Christ is a reflection of his disdain for their passivity. During
Christ's time in Gethsemane—a dark night of the soul that
preceded his crucifixion—the disciples whom he loved abandoned him out of fear for their own lives. In a legendary act of
betrayal, Judas Iscariot sold Jesus to the Roman officials and
thereby guaranteed his execution. Holden angrily holds the
disciples accountable for their disloyalty, even though his
classmate considers his criticism of Christ's apostles to be
sacrilegious.

By preferring the lunatic to the simpering disciples who fail
Jesus, Holden begins to articulate his own value system. While
Jesus is in agony on the last night of his life and while he asks
God to spare him or to give him strength to die nobly—the dis-
ciples sleep. During Christ's time of desperate need and terror,
Judas betrays him for thirty pieces of silver. When Judas leads
the soldiers to Jesus, Jesus says, "Judas, is it with a kiss that
you are betraying the Son of Man?" (Luke 22:48).

Known throughout the Gospels as "the one who betrayed
him," Judas repents too late: "When Judas, his betrayer, saw
that Jesus was condemned, he repented and brought back the
thirty pieces of silver to the chief priests and the elders. . .
Throwing down the pieces of silver in the temple, he departed;
and he went and hanged himself" (Matthew 27: 3, 5). The disciples courageously spread the Christian faith after Jesus died,

but during his life, as Holden notes, they were "about as much use to Him as a hole in the head."

The concept of the absurd is central to Existentialism, and profound ironies lie at the heart of the Bible as well. Much wisdom is paradoxical, something that the authors of the Bible, poet Emily Dickinson, and Salinger understand. In Mark 8:36 and Matthew 10:39, for example, we read: "For what will it profit them to gain the whole world and forfeit their life?" and "Those who find their life will lose it, and those who lose their life for my sake will find it."

A demand for justice and a challenge to complacency fuel *The Catcher in the Rye* and are at the heart of Holden's interest in madness, which is by definition behaving in a manner that seems counterintuitive to the majority. When Holden says he dislikes the disciples and would prefer to be the lunatic who lives in the graveyard, he refers specifically to "Legion," a man so named because he suffered from multiple personalities and lived as an outcast. Mark 5:3–5 describes Legion, a man abandoned by the townspeople:

> He lived among the tombs; and no one could restrain him any more, even with a chain; for he had often been restrained with shackles and chains, but the chains he wrenched apart, and the shackles he broke in pieces; and no one had the strength to subdue him. Night and day among the tombs and on the mountains he was always howling and bruising himself with stones.

After Jesus drives out the evil spirits that possess him, the townspeople come to the prophet in wonder: "They came to Jesus and saw the demoniac sitting there, clothed and in his right mind, the very man who had had the legion; and they were afraid" (Mark 5:15).

Too often characterized as a tale of immaturity, immorality, and juvenile angst, *The Catcher in the Rye* is really a portrait of a young man who struggles to make sense of his life and to understand the role of compassion and human agency in the midst of a Kafkaesque nightmare. Often calling himself "mad" or "crazy," Holden questions the purpose of life and reacts to the failure of human beings to act on one another's behalf. Furious with the passivity of the disciples and of those around him, Holden prefers a biblical figure who lived among the rocks and was considered insane over the disciples who abandoned Jesus when he needed them most.

Holden the Compassionate

An admittedly irrational compassion lies at the heart of Holden's emerging philosophy of life, and he understands that the world rarely rewards those who exhibit empathy and put themselves at risk to assist others. In spite of his sadness and confusion, he helps two nuns with their suitcases and worries because they can't go somewhere "swanky" for lunch (16, p. 149). He helps a child with her skate because "she didn't have any gloves on or anything and her hands were all red and cold" (16, p. 155). Although he misquotes the title of Robert Burns's poem "Comin' Thro' the Rye," the title of the novel itself refers to Holden's desire to rescue others before they hurt themselves:

> "Thousands of little kids, and nobody's around—nobody big, I mean—except me. And I'm standing on the edge of some crazy cliff. What I have to do, I have to catch everybody if they start to go over the cliff—I mean if they're running and they don't look where they're going I have to come out from somewhere and *catch* them. That's all I'd do all day. I'd just be the catcher in the rye and all. I know it's crazy, but that's the only thing I'd really like to be. I know it's crazy." (22, p. 224–25)

His love for and protection of Phoebe speak for themselves, providing even more evidence that Holden is at heart a person invested in the lives of others.

In addition to his belief in human compassion, Holden is concerned about equality and is conscious of what others might describe as universal law, which is defined as behavior that people generally believe to be acceptable, fair, and reasonable. He muses about how hard it is to be someone's roommate "if your suitcases are much better than theirs—if yours are really *good* ones and theirs aren't" (15, p. 142). He appears to feel guilty that he's privileged when others are struggling: "I hate it if I'm eating bacon and eggs or something and somebody else is only eating toast and coffee" (15, p. 143).

Just as importantly, Holden's compassion extends to nonhuman life as, throughout the novel, he worries about what happens to ducks (and fish) in winter. His concern about the lives of other creatures is not part of his adherence to a particular belief system, although Bonhoeffer, Kierkegaard, Tillich and others suggest a profound connection between a belief in God and service to those whom God created. For Holden, caring about the animals, fish, and fowl that populate the earth is similar to God's concern for the lilies of the field (Matthew 6:25–34): it indicates an awareness of the value of life and suggests that Holden is invested in "the least of these," a concept articulated often in the Bible. Matthew 25:40 reads, "Truly I tell you, just as you did it to one of the least of these who are members of my family, you did it to me" and Luke 12:6–7 reads, "Are not five sparrows sold for two pennies? Yet not one of them is forgotten in God's sight. But even the hairs of your head are all counted. Do not be afraid; you are of more value than many sparrows."

Holden tries to communicate his concern for nonhuman life in two conversations with taxi drivers in New York City. Talking to the first one, Holden asks: "You know those ducks in that lagoon right near Central Park South? That little lake? By any chance, do you happen to know where they go, the ducks, when it gets all frozen over? Do you happen to know, by any chance?" (9, p. 78). Later, he talks to another driver:

"'Hey, Horwitz,' I said. 'You ever pass by the lagoon in Central Park? Down by Central Park South? . . . Well, you know the ducks that swim around in it? In the springtime and all? Do you happen to know where they go in the wintertime, by any chance? . . . I mean does somebody come around in a truck or something and take them away, or do they fly away by themselves—go south or something?'" (12, pp. 106–07). Holden's anxiety about the plight of the ducks in winter is reminiscent of the concern Jesus expresses for the sparrows—and for the human beings who "are of more value than many sparrows." Holden may or may not identify with the ducks that have no shelter in the winter, but he empathizes with them and wants reassurance about their welfare.

Kierkegaard's *Fear and Trembling* is among numerous works by Christian philosophers that deal with this kind of individual subjective passion. It explores the biblical paradox that you must lose yourself in order to gain happiness, and focuses upon the roles of compassion, empathy, and human responsibility in civil society. It suggests that Holden's lack of respect for "Holy Joes" and passive onlookers is at the center of his philosophical development and his desire to understand the sign systems that surround him.

Holden expresses concern about helpless ducks on one of his most difficult nights: "I figured I'd go by that little lake and see what the hell the ducks were doing, see if they were around or not" (20, p. 199). His obsession with their welfare during his own dark night of the soul indicates a fledgling but rapidly developing understanding of his interconnectedness with the world.

For Holden as for the devoutly Catholic writer Flannery O'Connor, there is no option but to live passionately. Those who allow suffering are as culpable as those who actively perpetrate cruelty. In "The Displaced Person," O'Connor argues that the divine resides in the ordinary. Like Jesus, the Polish immigrant of her story is despised because he's different and is considered so dangerous to the status quo that he must be killed. Although one character actively causes the immigrant's death, others are complicit in the murder because they do not intervene. The immigrant is a child of God, someone who merits compassion and protection, and O'Connor's references to the "D.P." (displaced person) remove all doubt that he is the symbolic representation of the biblical Christ. In O'Connor's short story, those who do not protect the immigrant are analogous to the disciples who sleep as Jesus grieves in Gethsemane—and to those of us who protect ourselves by being safely passive.

Holden's Righteous Anger

Holden is a lunatic. Describing himself as crazy, Holden does not understand that "much madness is divinest sense" and that a passionate, caring life can appear aberrant to others. Loving Phoebe and worrying about ducks set him apart from those who prefer an unexamined life and who embrace conformity.

Holden also is an atheist. Nonetheless, Holden separates Jesus from organized Christianity, and his respect for the biblical Christ is evident. For example, Jesus cared about Judas, even though Judas betrayed him. "I said I'd bet a thousand bucks that Jesus never sent old Judas to Hell," Holden said; "I still would, too, if I had a thousand bucks. I think any one of the

Disciples would've sent him to Hell and all—and fast, too—but I'll bet anything Jesus didn't do it" (14, p. 131). Holden acknowledges the way in which Jesus embodies love and forgiveness but fails to understand that in doing so, Jesus, too, was an outcast, a lunatic.

Holden's admiration for Christ does not mitigate his distrust of religion as an institution. His disrespect for religion appears prominently when he talks about ministers and other representatives of the church:

> If you want to know the truth, I can't even stand ministers. The ones they've had at every school I've gone to, they all have these Holy Joe voices when they start giving their sermons. God, I hate that. I don't see why the hell they can't talk in their natural voice. They sound so phony when they talk." (14, p. 131)

Holden respects only those who exemplify a commitment to God in the way they live their lives: These people are not phony. Although he might not share their devotion to God, he appreciates their authenticity and wants more for them. Observing a group of nuns, Holden says:

> That's what I liked about those nuns. You could tell, for one thing, that they never went anywhere swanky for lunch. It made me so damn sad when I thought about it, their never going anywhere swanky for lunch or anything. (16, p. 149)

Tillich and other Christian philosophers argue that faith is not irrational; rather, it transcends reason. However, those who embody Christian values may appear to be lunatics or at least visibly out of sync with those around them. True faith evolves from a relationship with a divine being and is sustained by an act of will. Faith is all consuming. In *Dynamics of Faith,* Tillich writes:

> It transcends both the drives of the nonrational unconscious and the structures of the rational conscious. . . The ecstatic character of faith does not exclude its rational character although it is not identical with it, and it includes nonrational strivings without being identical with them. . ."Ecstasy" means "standing outside of oneself"—without ceasing to be oneself—with all the elements which are united in the personal center. (pp. 6–7)

The "personal center" is that which moors us and connects us to something higher than ourselves, and it is what Holden glimpses during his intermittent moments of awareness, even as he (and the reader) understand that he has a long way to go.

The Catcher in the Rye may be a chronicle of Holden's journey from innocence to experience but not from doubt to faith. This particular protagonist is not likely to profess a belief in God or move lockstep with members of any church. Although Holden is mired in cynicism and rage, he exhibits what Christian philosophers understand to be righteous anger. It's often prompted not by self-interest, but by his concern for the people and animals that inspire him to be a catcher in the rye.

Salinger's
Trash
and All

13
Censorship in the Rye

DONNA MARIE SMITH

The Catcher in the Rye is one of the most widely taught nov-els in high schools and one of the most frequently censored texts in the United States.

Ever since the book hit the number-one spot on the *New York Times* best-seller list for fiction when it was published in 1951, Jerome David Salinger's compelling work has stirred up controversy among parents, school boards, and religious groups concerned with the moral character of American young people. According to the American Library Association, this coming-of-age novel about prep school student Holden Caulfield's three-day adventure in Manhattan was listed as one of the top-ten most challenged books for 2009 due to offensive language, sex-ually explicit scenes, and unsuitability for young people.

Using first-person narration, the voice of Salinger's now iconic Holden comes through with the raw, angst-ridden feel-ings and observations of a teenager searching for his identity and struggling to make sense of and find a place in a confusing, materialistic society. It is this "voice" that stirs up fear and anx-iety in traditional, conservative sectors of modern American society.

Censorship is the suppression of speech, print, audio and visual materials, or symbolic forms of communication. In the United States, censorship has primarily taken two forms: polit-ical and cultural.

From the Revolutionary War to the Cold War, attempts were made by the government to suppress political and other ideas on the grounds of protecting national security. Newspapers—

and later, radio and television broadcasts—were often prevented from covering certain stories deemed unpatriotic, too radical, or too dangerous to the nation's concerns. The type of censorship primarily practiced in modern-day America focuses on cultural morés and ideas. Book-banning attempts and challenges to a book's inclusion in a public or school library, or into a classroom curriculum, mostly stem from individuals, religious groups, or school boards. Since its publication, Salinger's classic remains a perennial target of would-be censors.

On Holden's Liberty

Congress shall make no law respecting an establishment of religion, or prohibiting the free exercise thereof; or abridging the freedom of speech, or of the press; or the right of people peaceably to assemble, and to petition the Government for a redress of grievances.

— United States Constitution, Amendment I, December 15th, 1791

In laying the groundwork of the fledgling republic, the Founding Fathers of the United States emphasized the importance of freedom of speech by positioning it first in the Constitution's "Bill of Rights." They regarded this principle as the hallmark of individual liberty from which all other rights followed.

As a veteran of the Normandy campaign and an eyewitness to the horrors of the German concentration camps during World War II, Salinger fought for these cherished freedoms for people not just in his homeland but for those living in nations that valued similar principles. The irony of *Catcher* becoming the focus of many fervent book-banning attempts despite its author having served in a war against the Nazis—who used book-banning as a tool for advancing their agenda—is something that would have deeply disturbed Salinger's teenage protagonist. Holden would probably call all those adults who tried to keep the book out of their children's hands a "bunch of phonies."

One of the pre-eminent philosophers who stressed the importance of free speech in a democratic society was John Stuart Mill (1806–1873). Mill was especially interested in the ideas of liberty that helped to shape the nascent American republic, as well as spark the French Revolution (1789–1799). He wrote a number of works, including his book on freedom, *On Liberty*.

This groundbreaking treatise outlined Mill's vision of a productive, civilized society. He felt that both a government and its citizens should be tolerant of an individual's opinions and beliefs, because a balance between governmental authority and civil liberty is critical for a democracy to thrive.

Mill would have agreed with *The Catcher*'s defenders that readers have a right to check out the book from a library or study it in a classroom. Mill thought that political leaders should allow for the free exchange of political and religious ideas among individuals. Freedom of speech, the press, and thought, Mill believed, were central to a fruitful, just society. However, he explained that these liberties have a limitation: "The only purpose for which power can rightfully be exercised over any member of civilized community, against his will, is to prevent harm to others."[1]

This is known as the "Harm Principle." It holds that we can limit the exercise of someone's rights, including free speech, when those actions cause harm to others. A common example of harmful speech is of a person, say one of Holden's Pencey classmates, jokingly shouting "Fire!" in the school auditorium during assembly. This could cause panic, leading the students and teachers to push each other or get trampled.

In this case, the headmaster has a moral obligation to punish such irresponsible behavior. He should probably give the student detention or expel him, depending upon the extent of the damages to the room or the injuries to the kids. By citing the "Harm Principle" as a standard, the headmaster can provide concrete reasons why the prankster did not have a right to speak freely. He can show how the people in the auditorium were harmed by the prank. On the whole, the right of the Pencey students and faculty to be safe and free of physical injury outweighs the prankster's right to say whatever he wants.

Revealing classified national security or military information is also a type of "speech" that could be harmful and subjected to charges of treason or reckless endangerment. For

---

[1] *On Liberty*, Barnes and Noble, 2004, p. 10.

example, the 1953 espionage trial in which Americans Julius and Ethel Rosenberg were executed for passing atomic secrets to the Soviets and the more recent 2003 "Plamegate" incident in which *Washington Post* columnist Robert Novak compromised Valerie Plame's secret identity as a CIA agent are instances where an individual's spoken or written words were detrimental to the nation or to a fellow citizen.

Holden Offends Grown-Ups

Some philosophers felt that Mill's "Harm Principle" failed to adequately address why certain forms of speech should be limited. The American political and social philosopher Joel Feinberg (1926–2004) expanded on Mill's theory and stated that bigoted and prejudicial statements, blasphemous words, and pornographic expressions can offend an individual or group of people. Called the "Offense Principle," this standard attempts to measure how speech affects the sensibilities of a person or community. Feinberg classifies obscene words into three categories: "religious profanities," "vulgarities," and "impolite words."[2]

Some parents and religious groups have considered that Salinger's words are blasphemous. They feel that the book insults their God and religion. Throughout the novel, Holden uses phrases like "Jesus Christ" (4, p. 39), "Jesus H. Christ" (4, p. 41), and "for Chrisssake" (4, p. 40) in the course of a normal conversation with his classmates. His speech is also peppered with vulgarities such as "crap" (2, p. 21) and "backasswards" (6, p. 53) and impolite words like "son of a bitch" (3, p. 32) and "bastard" (20, p. 194). Feinberg theorizes that a case can be made for limiting obscene speech depending on the speaker's intentions and the scope of the offensive remarks.

Some people, though, don't intend offense when using obscenities. In *Catcher*, Salinger uses vulgar and profane words in order to portray realistically the speech of a teenager. He also wants Holden's language to symbolize his dissatisfaction with the phoniness of society and his dislike of phony people. Salinger doesn't let his characters speak obscenities for the sake of offending his readers or simply for shock value.

---

[2] *The Moral Limits of the Criminal Law: Offense to Others*, Oxford University Press, 1985, Volume 2, pp. 190–91.

As Feinberg explains, while some people use obscenities out of disrespect for others, some, like Salinger, use it "habitually to reject the prevailing norms of propriety generally, to express a certain attitude toward life, and to convey an image of cynical tough-mindedness" (p. 251). That about sums up Holden: the cynical teenager trying to be an adult in the big city despite the phoniness and crassness he encounters during his three-day journey. Feinberg goes on to say that "such persons have no reverence for 'bullshit stuff;' they see through sentimentality, patriotic cant, and the like" (p. 252). On the whole, Salinger uses obscene language as a literary device to signify the novel's theme of how the conservative, materialistic American society of the 1950s stifled individual expression and creativity. Basically, he was using "bullshit" to speak out against "bullshit.

Most of the furor surrounding Salinger's book has focused on its use of profane language. Concerned parents and educators have pointed to the passage where Holden agrees with his friend Sally that "he probably is a sacrilegious atheist" (18, p. 178) as a primary example of why the book is anti-Christian. Fundamentalist Christian organizations and political New Right groups like televangelist Jerry Falwell's Moral Majority felt that the text was an affront to their religious values and promoted secular humanism, a philosophy espoused by contemporary thinkers such as Albert Camus (1913–1960) which endorsed reason instead of religion or God as the guide to leading an ethical, just life.

The Moral Majority and others feared that children would emulate Holden's profane way of thinking and speaking. Some of these conservative religious groups formed in response to teachers incorporating Salinger's and other books into their curricula. Yet, Holden doesn't use profanity to offend anyone. He's just talking like a typical American teenager. As Kenneth Slawenski explains, *Catcher* provides a view of the world "as seen through the lens of an adolescent and rendered in a language true to the narrator's location and age."[3] Salinger, in letting him speak this way, gives Holden a voice more authentic than one sanitized for possible censors.

These objections to the vulgarity and profanity of *Catcher*, and complaints about their offensiveness, might not always be

---

[3] *J.D. Salinger: A Life*, Random House, 2010, p. 205.

the real motivation behind efforts to censor it. In an extensive and fascinating study of the censorship of Salinger's novel, scholar Pamela Hunt Steinle theorizes that parents and religious groups in the 1950s felt that Holden and his misadventures threatened American society. She identifies the National Organization for Decent Literature (NODL) as the first group to formally contest the book's value.[4]

NODL was made up of parents and "concerned citizens" who led the first "well-organized nationwide effort to censor high school reading materials in general." Established in 1938 by the Catholic Bishops of the United States, the group set out to rid the nation of immoral and unpatriotic printed materials, targeting magazines, comic books, textbooks, and novels.

At the heart of Steinle's thesis is the Cold War and the social morés of post-war America. She takes a look at how the fear of nuclear annihilation, as well as Senator Joseph McCarthy's persecution of alleged Communist sympathizers during the late 1940s and 1950s, led some Americans to espouse a conservative, patriotic fervor which precluded any political or cultural dissent among fellow citizens. Many parents and religious leaders loathed the explicit language and mentions of sex in Holden's story and viewed the book as a subversive attempt to turn kids into Communists. They were fearful that kids would copy the wayward Holden.

There is no evidence that Salinger was wrting the book to recruit young people into the Communist Party, nor that the author himself was in any way involved with Communism. Nothing in Salinger's background indicates any unpatriotic inclinations or associations. After graduating from the Valley Forge Military Academy in Pennsylvania, he focused primarily on writing and establishing a literary career. During World War II, he earned five battle stars and the Presidential Unit Citation for valor, and he served in the Army Signal Corps and the Army Counter Intelligence Corps, which investigated personnel for treasonous activities.

The manner in which Salinger conducted himself during the war and in later civilian life reveals no anti-American activities. His military service record, professional dealings,

---

[4] *In Cold Fear: The Catcher in the Rye Censorship Controversies and the Cold War in America*, Ohio State University Press, 2002, pp. 73–80.

and secluded personal lifestyle show that he cherished American values such as personal freedom and privacy above all else.

If a Censor Catches Books

Another possible exception to John Stuart Mill's belief that no one should interfere with an individual's liberties is in the case of minors. Parents, school boards, and religious groups who have tried to ban *Catcher in the Rye* from schools have said that Holden's obscene language and depraved descriptions of his trip to New York could cause *harm* to impressionable young people and thus ultimately to the moral fabric of society. Parents and members of school boards worried that students who read the book will emulate Holden: use swear words, drop out of school, engage with prostitutes and other undesirables of society, get drunk, or use the Lord's name in vain. They thought Holden was a terrible role model for their kids and their neighbor's kids.

The fear of losing control over what their child would become, what society would become, is why parents and "concerned citizens" challenge works like *The Catcher in the Rye*. This fear is the primary underlying philosophical and psychological motivation behind their censorship attempts. Examples of these challenge range from small groups like several parents who, in 1977, told the board of education in Pittsgrove Township, New Jersey, that the book "promoted premarital sex, homosexuality, and perversion"[5] to formally-organized censorship groups.

In 1961, a group in Oklahoma City tried to prevent a book wholesaler, the Mid-Continent News Company, from carrying books like *Catcher*. The group's efforts led to a hearing with the state legislature. During the proceedings, "members of the group parked a 'Smutmobile' outside the capital building and displayed the novel with others." The company eventually caved to this high-profile public pressure.

Throughout Holden's narrative of his time at Pencey and his trip to Manhattan, he uses "filthy" words in recounting his

---

[5] Dawn B. Sova, *Banned Books: Literature Suppressed on Social Grounds*, Facts on File, 2006, p. 86.

various "vulgar" activities. While in the city, he goes to a bar where he drinks alcohol and smokes cigarettes. He observes a man "feeling up his date" (12, p. 112) and sees a woman with "very big knockers" (12, p. 112). He also has a prostitute come up to his hotel room (although he sends her away with his virginity still intact). In many of the challenges to *Catcher*, parents have tried to remove the book from school libraries or classroom curricula because they deemed Holden's words and exploits offensive and immoral. Despite the potential educational value of the book, the challengers did not want impressionable children hearing about Holden's scandalous adventures.

Legal judgments in the United States Supreme Court often failed to reach a consensus in cases involving free speech and the First Amendment rights of minors. The ongoing struggle between societal norms and individual liberties was seen most clearly in the important 1976 case *Pico v. Board of Education, Island Trees Union Free School District.* A board of education in a Long Island, New York, school district had tried to remove several books, including Kurt Vonnegut's 1969 science fiction novel *Slaughterhouse Five,* from a junior-high-school library and a high-school English class. Five students sued the school district, alleging that the school board had based its decision solely on passages that conflicted with its members' values. While Salinger's novel was not one of the challenged books in the *Pico* case, the reasons why the school board wanted to remove these works were similar to those for wanting to ban *Catcher*.

Some of the justices felt that the schoolchildren lacked the intellectual capacity to understand the variety of disparate ideas presented in the challenged books, while others thought that the school board did not have the right to impose its personal views on the students. Writing the plurality opinion, Justice William J. Brennan, Jr. ruled in favor of the students, concluding that school boards can't remove books from a school library or prevent teachers from teaching a book just because they disagree with or dislike the ideas contained within them.

The National Council of Teachers of English recognized that, while not all censorship attempts resulted in legal action, the prevalence of requests for removal of books in school libraries and classrooms remained a constant concern for educators and librarians. In 1981, the Council adopted "The

Students' Right to Read," a bill of rights which expanded on the right of free inquiry guaranteed by the First Amendment. They held that the freedom to explore a wide variety of ideas is central to a democratic education.

Plato Would Censor Holden

Parents, school boards, and legal scholars are not the only ones who have struggled to reach a balance between deeply held social and religious values and a child's right to free expression or the receipt of information. Modern-day proponents of free speech believe that school officials, parents, and special-interest groups should not prevent children from reading any particular book. One of the most stringent censors, especially when it came to children's education, was the ancient Greek philosopher Plato (around 427–347 B.C.).

In the *Republic*, one of the most influential works of Western philosophy, Plato explains his position concerning the limitations of a child's education. He believes that children should be safeguarded from any fictional tales that are immoral and blasphemous. Even Homer's epic poems the *Iliad* and the *Odyssey* are not exempt from the strict educational guidelines he proposes that call for omitting any questionable lines when reciting literature to a young audience.

While Plato does not advocate the outright banning of Homer's poetry, he suggests removing any passages that portray the gods and heroes of ancient Greece in an unfavorable light, such as having sex with one another or with mortals. Like the would-be censors of *Catcher,* Plato would consider Salinger's book to have no educational value. He would not want the children of Athens to hear Holden's story. Since he believes that children should learn how to be virtuous and should strive to be like the gods and heroes, he would not want them to be like Holden nor any of the adults in Holden's life. Perhaps Holden's sister Phoebe, who is wise and virtuous despite her young age, would be an acceptable role model for his students.

Another idea that Plato stressed in the *Republic* is that teachers should protect those in their care from the "lies" of literature. He felt that "a young person cannot judge what is allegorical and what is literal; anything that he receives into his mind at that age is likely to become indelible and unalterable." [6] Parents, school boards, and religious leaders who challenged Salinger's take on modern youth would agree with Plato that Holden's voice had no place in their children's education. Teenagers are just too impressionable to distinguish what's real from what's imaginary, and right behavior from wrong.

Holden and the Marketplace of Ideas

As one of the most progressive Western thinkers who advanced the principles of free speech, John Stuart Mill concluded that the only way for a society to thrive was to allow for a variety of opinions and values. He believed that an individual should be free to speak or write about politics, religion, or social issues without fear of punishment. A society that values "life, liberty, and the pursuit of happiness" can only benefit from multiple opinions and values.

Mill provides three reasons why free speech should not be suppressed by a government or by special-interest groups:

- **A censored opinion may be true and the accepted opinion false.**

- **Even truth needs to be challenged and tested.**

- **There's probably some degree of truth in all opinions.**

Sometimes the prevailing opinion or value needs to be challenged, sometimes preserved; but only by evaluating and re-evaluating long-established ideas can the truth be revealed.

Mill built his theories of liberty upon the works of two influential seventeenth-century figures: the English poet John Milton (1608–1674) and the philosopher John Locke (1632–1704). John Milton, author of *Paradise Lost*, advocated free expression in his 1644 essay *Areopagitica: A Speech for the Liberty of Unlicensed Printing*.

Written as an indictment of the British Parliament's "Licensing Order Act of 1643," which placed an undue burden on publishing and disseminating of materials, the essay decried the act's harsh censorship measures. The law called for

---

[6] *Republic*, Barnes and Noble, 2004, p. 65.

the licensing of a text prior to publication and the registration with a central agency of all people involved in the authorship and printing of materials. What's more, the government could arrest and imprison any author or printer whose publications were deemed offensive.

Fortunately, the government of Great Britain, the United States, and other democratic societies can no longer fine or imprison authors like Salinger, his editor, or the owners of his publishing house, Little, Brown, and Company, since protections like the English Bill of Rights (1689) and the American Bills of Rights (1791) are in place.

One of the most important concepts that came from Milton's eloquent tract was the notion of the "marketplace of ideas" as the building block of a free society. Like John Stuart Mill after him, Milton used this concept as an allegory for the free exchange of opinions among free people. He even based the title of the essay, *Areopagitica*, on the name of a market in ancient Athens where citizens gathered to discuss ideas and the courts met to decide laws.

Milton maintained that the government's legal and monetary restrictions on the dissemination of printed materials hampered the growth of the nation. Only by giving its citizens the right to read and to think about a variety of ideas and to discuss and write freely can an individual, a nation, or a civilization expand and evolve. Otherwise, we'd still be thinking that the Sun and planets revolve around the Earth!

The philosopher John Locke also influenced John Stuart Mill's theories of intellectual freedom, as well as the principles set forth in both the Declaration of Independence and the Constitution of United States. Locke wrote several important essays concerning the rights of free expression, as well as of religious preference. In his *Letters Concerning Toleration* (1689), he advocated the rights of people to practice the religion of their choice, and in his *Two Treatises of Government* (1689), he explained that people had natural and equal rights to "life, liberty, and property."

Holden's Right to Free Expression

John Milton, John Stuart Mill, Joel Feinberg, and modern-day advocates of civil rights, view freedom of speech as an essential human liberty. In order to have a healthy, flourishing society, individuals have to be allowed unrestricted access to ideas and information, including those which are unpopular or different from the norms of a given community. While the outright banning of books by governments is rare in the democratic societies of today, individuals and groups persist in trying to get books removed from classrooms or library shelves. Even sixty years later, *Catcher in the Rye* continues to be a target for those who do not understand its artistic and educational value. Many parents and religious groups still regard it as obscene and blasphemous.

A recent controversy surrounding a newly-published, sanitized version of Mark Twain's *The Adventures of Huckleberry Finn*—another American classic targeted for its offensive language—points to the reason why censorship is so insidious.[7] We can't eradicate the horrors of our country's racism as depicted by Twain (this edition replaced the "n-word" with the word "slave"), no more than we can the problems faced by an adolescent on the verge of adulthood. Literature is a microcosm of society, and we can learn from the stories that we read. By having access to a variety of ideas as portrayed in books like these, we can learn how things were and how things should be. If someone erased all the bad language that Salinger uses, just as Holden erased the bad word on the wall in Phoebe's school, then would the story have the same impact or meaning? Would we still understand Holden's struggle to reconcile the authenticity and purity of childhood with the phoniness and messiness of adulthood? Most likely, the answer is "no."

Salinger's novel remains widely read despite numerous attempts to ban it. By using teenage vernacular, Salinger lets Holden Caulfield speak to young adults in a way that matters. Strip away the curse words, the smoking and drinking, and the curiosity about sex, and Holden's story is the story of all children on the threshold of adulthood. Actually, keep all of that, and readers learn that Holden is just like them. He's like any young person trying to discover their place in a phony and often confusing world.

---

[7] Alan Gribben, *Mark Twain's Adventures of Tom Sawyer and Huckleberry Finn: The New South Edition*, New South, 2011.

14

The Case Against Salinger's Trash

Claudia Franziska Brühwiler

You've been selected to serve on the Jury in this case of various plaintiffs against *The Catcher in the Rye* by J.D. Salinger. The book is charged with being:

1. *anti*-American, anti-authority, anti-Catholic, and anti-white

2. *immoral*

3. *defamatory* to the disabled, to minorities, and to women

4. *Communist*

5. *an advocate of* alcoholism, dishonesty, homosexuality, and prostitution

6. *profane.*

Some of these charges resound in the menacing words of Ackley, Holden Caulfield's former colleague at Pencey Prep, when he says: "Listen, I don't care what you say about *me* or anything, but if you start making cracks about my goddam re*lig*ion, for Chrissake—" (7, p. 65).

In a similar spirit and more in tune with the plaintiffs' concerns, the Educational Research Analysts, a Christian organization reviewing textbooks since 1961,[1] drafted a list of criteria under which a book should be banned from schools.

---

[1] The organization still exists: http://www.textbookreviews.org/.

On this list, *The Catcher in the Rye* can be found in Category 43, "trash."

Today, you are to decide whether the book should be banned from libraries and school curricula on the grounds of its having adverse effects on readers. In other words, you'll first have to determine whether literature can have any impact on the reader at all.

Secondly, you are to decide whether the book at hand has a positive or a negative effect on its readers.

Thirdly, if you find that the book has a negative effect on its readers, you're to judge whether this warrants a ban. In order to reach a just decision, you will first hear a brief history of the case. Subsequently, the plaintiffs will present their case for a book ban. The defense will then have the chance to counter these charges. At the end, you are called to consider and weigh the evidence presented by the parties, including the testimony of all the witnesses who will appear before you.

You alone will determine whether to believe any witness and the extent to which you believe them. You are reminded of the oath which you have taken as a juror. If you follow that oath, and try the issues without fear or prejudice, bias or sympathy, you will arrive at a true and just verdict.

The Case

The Catcher in the Rye was first published in 1951. In 2009, the American Library Association still ranked it sixth on a list of— not the most read or most popular school books, but—the most challenged books. It was by no means the first time that the book appeared in this listing; it has been a censor's favorite for decades.[2] Nor was Holden's story the only modern classic to meet such opposition: it shared and still shares this honor with other classics such as Harper Lee's *To Kill a Mocking Bird,* and Alice Walker's *The Color Purple*, as well as rather recent bestsellers such as Stephenie Meyer's *Twilight* series.

But who challenges the account of Holden Caulfield's trip to and through New York? It is groups and individuals of consid-

---

[2] You can find the ranking on the website of the American Library Association as well as other useful information on book bans in the United States: http://www.ala.org.

erable diversity, yet with similar preoccupations, as a—starkly abbreviated—chronology of challenges against *The Catcher in the Rye* reveals:

1956   The National Organization for Decent Literature, a Roman Catholic pressure group, declared the novel objectionable. Holden might sneer: "Catholics are always trying to find out if you're a Catholic." (15, p. 146)

1960   In Tulsa, Oklahoma, a teacher was fired because he had assigned *The Catcher in the Rye* to an eleventh-grade English class.

1978   In Issaquah, Washington, a watchful citizen tabulated 785 "profanities" in the novel and launched a campaign, which resulted in Holden's story being banned from local high schools. Holden might comment: "So I got the ax." (1, p. 6)

1987   In Napoleon, North Dakota, parents and the local chapter of the Knights of Columbus, a Catholic fraternal service organization, pressured a high school board to remove the book from the mandatory English reading list.

1997   In Brunswick, Georgia, a student challenged the book, although unsuccessfully.
In Marysville, California, the school superintendent removed the book from the required reading list.

Among the plaintiffs, we find both parents and pupils, school representatives and religious circles, as well as worried citizens assembled. Now that the plaintiffs have been identified, let us hear how they perceive the case!

Evidence Offered by the Plaintiffs

The plaintiffs do not wish to further elaborate on the charges that have been presented by the Court at the outset of the trial, as they are not at the center of the question presented to you, Member of the Jury. Instead, their evidence shall prove that a book such as *The Catcher in the Rye* can have a negative impact on its readers. In the course of the following argument, you will hear the testimony of eminent expert witnesses.

Exhibit 1: the first paperback edition of the book. While today's readers have to actually *read The Catcher in the Rye* to capture its allegedly offensive content, in 1953, readers of the first paperback edition could tell from the cover what to expect: "This unusual book may shock you," it announced, and further nourished this particular expectation with the depiction of young Holden standing in front of a dubious nightclub with a woman at his side, probably a prostitute, who is lighting a cigarette. Dangers await the young protagonist, even more dangers await the reader, is the message of the cover. Holden himself explains why the reader is at great risk while he watches the "perverts" in the other rooms at the Edmont Hotel: "The trouble was, that kind of junk is sort of fascinating to watch, even if you don't want it to be" (9, p. 81).

Fascination goes, in the eyes of the plaintiffs, hand in hand with influence: "that kind of junk" (9, p. 81) may in the end influence you—very negatively. Evidence, Members of the Jury?

Exhibit 2: a copy of the book with a handwritten dedication in it, *"To Holden Caulfield. From Holden Caulfield. This is my statement."* Exhibit 2 was found in the pocket of Mark David Chapman, who, equally obsessed with *The Catcher* and *The Beatles*, shot John Lennon on December 8th, 1980.

Admittedly we, the plaintiffs, would be phonies if we insisted that the book could turn every reader into an assassin. Our point is, however, that the book has a detrimental influence, particularly on young readers, and that it's the plaintiffs' duty to protect their offspring from it. To further elaborate on this point, the plaintiffs call an expert witness: Plato (427–347 B.C.), philosopher and disciple of Socrates. He saw it as the duty of every just government to protect children from indecency—and he would have shared the plaintiffs' concern.

Although the "novel" as a genre had yet to be created in Plato's era, it's an example of what Plato called *mimetic* art. *Mimesis* means "imitation" and describes what Plato saw as the main function of art and poetry, namely to imitate the world as it is. Because literature as a mimetic art only imitates the world and the actors within, Plato believed it incapable of broadening our knowledge of anything. Since writers and poets rarely have first-hand knowledge of what they describe, they cannot provide the reader with true insight. One could liken Plato's distaste for mimetic art to Holden Caulfield's problem with actors: "I hate actors. They never act like people. They just think they do. . . . If an actor acts it out, I hardly listen. I keep worrying about whether he's going to do something phony every minute" (16, p. 152–53).

"So what?" the defense might want to interject—who would read Holden Caulfield's account in the hope of getting a sociological study of American boarding schools? In the case of *The Catcher in the Rye* it is indeed not possible pseudo-knowledge that worries the plaintiffs. We would rather want you, Member of the Jury, to focus on Plato's chief work *The Republic*, in which he outlined the ideal society. According to Plato, it would require guardians, who would be selected during early childhood and trained from the very beginning of their education in a guardian's virtues and duties. As guardians, they would protect the Republic against its enemies, but not abuse their strength and power to oppress the other citizens; instead, they would be loyal servants of their community.

Reflecting on the future guardians' education, Plato considered what these children should be allowed to read. In doing so, Plato contemplated literature's effects on its readers. He concluded that their curriculum had to be monitored carefully, for Plato found that mimetic art can have both negative and positive effects on the reader's mind. From Plato's perspective, a book like *The Catcher in the Rye* could have particularly adverse effects on future guardians and contravene an important virtue they should develop. Holden Caulfield mocks authorities, calls people of repute "phony," and repeatedly violates rules. In short, he would have set a bad example for the guardians, who were supposed to preserve the status quo and defend public order.

Plato would argue that it would be disastrous for the community if its guardians felt about Holden as he feels for his favorite books: "What really knocks me out is a book that, when you're all done reading it, you wish the author that wrote it was a terrific friend of yours and you could call him up on the phone whenever you felt like it" (3, p. 25). What would Holden advise a guardian to do if the latter ever doubted his or her superiors? The answer, as you will agree, would probably imperil society's order.

The plaintiffs believe that they have offered enough evidence to prove their case that *The Catcher in the Rye* should be banished from classrooms and school reading lists. Let's hear whether the defense has any convincing counter-arguments!

Evidence Offered by the Defense

The defense against banning *The Catcher in the Rye* will address mainly two claims: 1. that literature cannot teach us anything and 2. that literary works such as Holden's coming of age story are harmful. Plato's most famous disciple Aristotle (384–322 B.C.) had a more positive view of mimetic art and believed it to be "more philosophical" than history. Instead of simply showing what had happened, as history does, literature, Aristotle argued, shows what might have happened, what twists and turns life can take.[3]

The defense's second expert witness, contemporary American philosopher Martha C. Nussbaum (*1947) has further explored Aristotle's thought that literature can indeed teach us more—or, more precisely, something else—than history. In *Poetic Justice: The Literary Imagination and Public Life* (Beacon Press, 1995), Nussbaum argues that literature can have a lasting impact on readers' behavior, an emotional impact which can hardly be achieved by history or other types of scholarly texts. Literature, she writes, "summons powerful emotions, it disconcerts and puzzles" (p. 5). It exerts an emotive power over its readers and appeals to an innate human capacity she calls "fancy," a term she borrows from Charles Dickens.

Although Holden Caulfield is not exactly a fan of Dickens (1, p. 1, 18, p. 179), he would definitely agree that a writer's actual experience and expertise is never as important as his or her ability to incite a reader's imagination and evoke emotions. In this vein, Holden shares the opinion of his brother D.B. that actual military experience is not needed in order to convey an accurate impression of war's realities: "I remember Allie once asked him wasn't it sort of good that D.B. was in the war because he was a writer and it gave him a lot to write about and all. He made Allie go get his baseball mitt and then he

---

[3] See, in particular, Aristotle's *Poetics*.

asked him who was the best war poet, Rupert Brooke or Emily Dickinson. Allie said Emily Dickinson" (18, p. 182).

English poet Rupert Chawner Brooke (1887–1915) died while serving in the British naval force, while American poet Emily Dickinson (1830–1886) hardly ever left her home. Still, both army trained D.B. and the relatively inexperienced Allie agree that it's the poetry of this mysterious spinster rather than the words of the worldly Brooke which captures best the realities of war and violence.

According to Nussbaum, literature evokes emotions, one of which is particularly important to our life as citizens: compassion, or "fellow-feeling." The latter term was coined by our next witness, the Scottish philosopher Adam Smith (1723–1790), who most of you, Members of the Jury, might know best for his inquiry into the mechanisms of markets in his classic *The Wealth of Nations*, but he also wrote about morality.

In *Theory of Moral Sentiments* (1759), Smith describes the concept of the impartial or judicious spectator. The judicious spectator is the ideal combination of reason and emotion. According to Smith, the judicious spectator can not only imagine himself—vividly, as Nussbaum stresses—in another person's situation, but simultaneously perceive the situation "with his present reason and judgment" (p. 76). Nussbaum refers to this idea when she describes how literature instills compassion: by assuming the position of the "judicious spectator," she argues, the reader is able to comprehend the inner plight of a person and feelings he never experienced himself. In other words, individuals who read will be able to simultaneously take the stand of the rational observer, the spectator, and of the person concerned. Thus, the reader is forced to assume an outside and inside perspective at the same time. Literature has a moral effect by instilling in its readers compassion, Nussbaum argues, which eventually turns them into better citizens.

"A minority view!" some might interject. Not at all. Martha Nussbaum's views are shared by American philosopher Richard Rorty (1931–2007). In *Contingency, Irony, and Solidarity* (Cambridge University Press, 1989), Rorty argued that citizens can only grasp the nature of current problems by reading novels along with philosophic works. Just like Martha Nussbaum, Richard Rorty believes that literature gives individuals insight into ways of living that are otherwise inaccessible, insights which alter individuals' moral disposition and teach compassion. The latter is key to achieving the main goal of liberalism. This goal consists for Rorty in the reduction of cruelty, an idea he adopts from the philosopher Judith Shklar (1928–1992).

In her influential essay "The Liberalism of Fear" (*Political Thought and Political Thinkers*, University of Chicago Press, 1998), Judith Shklar bases the legitimacy of liberalism on the idea of the greatest evil, a *summum malum*, which she identifies as cruelty and the fear of cruelty: as different as we all may be from each other, as much as culture and heritage may set us apart, we all fear cruelty. A just regime thus has to guarantee that no one's afraid of systematic cruelty. According to Richard Rorty, literature heightens our awareness of cruelty in two ways: firstly, it makes us more sensitive to cruelty suffered by people whom we usually ignore. Secondly, reading makes us aware of the cruelty of which we ourselves might be capable.

Defense: Conclusions from the Evidence

The jury might wonder, "In what way should Holden Caulfield's account make anyone more sensitive to cruelty?"

As teenagers, many of us often felt misunderstood; some of us still do as adults—but few may have been so frequently misunderstood as J.D. Salinger's anti-hero. Hidden behind his inappropriate, offensive language and his contemptuous attitude, Holden is a caring, vulnerable adolescent who struggles with the hypocrisy and the contradictions of his environs. Holden is only in his *"mind . . .* the biggest sex maniac you ever saw" (9, p. 81); he's actually a sensitive young man, his dearest wish being to protect the innocent and "just be the catcher in the rye and all" (22, p. 225). Holden's desire is very similar to the plaintiffs' effort to keep their children from reading "trash"; recall his efforts to clean his sister's school of verbal smut:

> Somebody'd written 'Fuck you' on the wall. It drove me damn near crazy. I thought how Phoebe and all the other little kids would see it, and how they'd wonder what the hell it meant, and then finally some dirty kid would tell them—all cockeyed, naturally—what it meant, and how they'd all think about it and maybe even worry about it for a couple of days. I kept wanting to kill whoever'd written it. (25, p. 260)

Both the plaintiffs and Holden want to protect children from ugliness and the other bad things in life; they want to preserve their innocence and purity. However, the plaintiffs and, of course, the rest of the readership would first have to reconsider their own position and realize, as Holden Caulfield did, that they could not act forever as "the catcher in the rye":

> That's the whole trouble. You can't ever find a place that's nice and peaceful, because there isn't any. You may think there is, but once you get there, when you're not looking, somebody'll sneak up and write 'Fuck you' right under your nose. (25, p. 264)

Through Holden's eyes, the plaintiffs would also learn to see the conventions of this society differently. His disgust with the phoniness, pretenses and superficiality of the adult world invites a discussion of everyday morality and ethics, his eventual expression of compassion for the phonies even more so. Finally, Holden's account mirrors the fears and angst of a generation that grew up during the Cold War and was constantly reminded of the impending danger of a nuclear war: "Anyway, I'm sort of glad they've got the atomic bomb invented. If there's another war, I'm going to sit right the hell on top of it. I'll volunteer for it, I swear to God I will" (18, p. 183). We, today's readers, live in a different world, but are confronted with comparable existential threats. Holden may offer us a chance of introspection, a chance to see our own fears through his eyes and reflect on alternative ways to confront them.

The Catcher in the Rye is one of the works of literature that, to quote Martha Nussbaum, promotes "identification and emotional reaction, requiring us to see and to respond to many things that may be difficult to confront" (p. 6). At first sight, Holden seems to be just another spoiled, dissatisfied youth who exerts a destructive influence on his environs and succumbs to his immediate desire to loath and waste away. A second, prolonged look reveals the young man's sensitivity, as he points out society's superficiality, its contradictions and complexity. Holden's account is one of the many mirrors of our world that we should not be afraid to look into—don't you agree, Member of the Jury?

The defense rests.

Verdict

You have heard the evidence, you have heard different expert opinions. Now it's up to you, Member of the Jury, to reach a verdict.

15
Is Holden Mentally Ill?

MICHAEL CUNDALL

Why does Holden want to be a catcher in the rye? He says, "I know it's crazy, but that's the only thing I'd really like to be. I know it's crazy" (22, p. 225).

Holden's dream seems nonsensical: heartfelt but nuts. One couldn't do that, as no such profession really exists. How would he live and support himself? Where could he do this? Given that many of Holden Caulfield's other claims throughout the novel turn out to be false or dubious at best, the fact that he has wild swings in behavior and mood (his general crumbiness), the traumatic effects of his witnessing the suicide of a classmate and his near-descent into madness as he crosses the streets and comes ever closer to walking into traffic, many readers have thought that Holden suffered from sort of mental disease or disorder.

But the problem is that Holden always seems to come back from his nadirs. He recovers and moves on. And at the end of the novel his attitude toward his story seems fairly nonchalant. Is he just telling us about a couple of bad days or is this just another brief moment of lucidity and normalcy before another episode occurs?

While it's not easy to diagnose someone as having a mental illness based on a snapshot of a few days, it doesn't seem a stretch to believe that Holden Caulfield was, in some meaningful way, suffering from a mental disorder or problem. While the ultimate answer to whether or not Caulfield has a mental disorder is probably not something that can adequately be resolved (we can't give a good diagnosis on only a few days observation), the question about whether Holden is mentally ill is a tantalizing one. But first we need to get clear on what it means to be mentally ill? Are mental disorders psychological, physical or both?

What Is a Crumby Mental Disorder?

Many of us have known someone who has been diagnosed with a mental disorder. Some people suffer from mild forms such as depression or social anxiety, whereas others may have debilitating phobias or suffer from severe manic depression or schizophrenia. Even depression and social anxiety can become debilitating. Thus it seems that the term "mental disorder" can be applied to a wide variety of conditions ranging from mild to major, from the level of nuisance to severe disorder, from a mild tick to severe autism.

And having or suffering from a mental disorder can have important consequences as well. People can miss work, lose jobs, threaten or ruin friendships and, as with Holden, end up bouncing from school to school and really straining family relationships. Mental disorder is serious and has become more prevalent, if the recent increase in prescription drugs for mental disorders like depression is any indication. So, in addition to our interest in deciding whether Holden has a mental disorder, the fact that most of us will end up dealing in some way with a mental disorder in our lives makes it important that we have a strong concept of mental disorder.

The name "mental disorder" provides a nice starting point into understanding what's going on when one suffers from a condition like depression or bipolar disorder. A mental disorder implies a disordered mind; not a mind unkempt like old Spencer's room (or Spencer himself), but a mind unable to perform in a normal fashion. This lack of order impedes the sufferer's ability to successfully accomplish things in his or her daily life.

Clinicians have often described the condition of a mental disorder as a "meaningful break with reality." The behaviors, ideas, and feelings of the person have created a situation where she simply does not or cannot interact with her life or people within it in a normal and productive way. Someone suffering from a mental disorder may mistake her hallucinations for reality (delusions). She may believe the person to whom she's talking is real, but not the actual person she knows; she believes the other person is a doppleganger (Capgras Syndrome).

Some people may feel bad or "down-in-the-dumps" and as a result perform poorly in their jobs, or derive no satisfaction from their personal lives (depression). Others may be unable to recognize familiar faces and thereby are unable to interact in normal ways (prosopagnosia). While there are a host of various mental disorders that we could study, ranging from the popular child's disorder of attention deficit disorder to cases of depression or Alzheimer's in adults, let's begin by comparing two cases of mental disorder: one familiar, depression, and the other less so, prosopagnosia.

Holden's Crumbiness and Mistaking a Wife for a Hat

Let's assume for a moment that Holden's depressed. At the very least he seems sort of out if it. Intuitively, depression fits the concept of mental disorder as a failure of the mind to properly function in normal activities and Holden seems certainly unable to do behave in a "normal" fashion. Depressives often can't get out of bed or make their way to their jobs as they may not feel such activities to be "worth it." Or if they can muster the energy to get going, they are slow to complete projects or they draw no satisfaction in the acts.

If Holden's depressed, his failures as the fencing team's "goddam manager" might be a telltale sign (1, p. 6). For a depressed person relationships and familiar activities no longer give the rewards they once did, or now feel like work. Holden certainly avoids his parents because he's often in trouble and they seem to him too far away from him. But even his relationship with his beloved sister Phoebe can cause him discomfort when he reflects on his behavior toward her. For a person with depression, overall output in life is reduced relative to his or her typical day to day activities. This certainly seems the case with Holden. The causes of depression are various but typically we see some major psychological event such as the loss of a loved one or experiencing a traumatic event (such as a brother dying or witnessing a suicide). We also often find an imbalance, which seems to imply disorder, of neurochemicals in the brain. These contribute to causing depression and can be treated with therapy and certain medications.

Compare the case of depression to prosopagnosia: the condition of being unable to recognize faces. The disorder of prosopagnosia, made famous by the renowned neurologist Oliver Sacks (about whom the movie *Awakenings* with Robin Williams and Robert DeNiro was made), renders a person unable to recognize faces. They simply don't see faces as uniform things in their visual field. When you and I see a face, we see them *as* faces. A person with prosopagnosia may see eyes, or a nose or a mouth, but they cannot put those things together into a face that he or she can recognize. Often people with prosopagnosia will mistake people for other things as in the case of a man who mistook his wife for a hat—when leaving a doctor's office he reached for what he took to be his hat, but instead grabbed his wife's face (apparently a typical behavior for this man).[1] This is a case of a mental disorder in that the mind is not working in the typical fashion allowing normal face recognition. The inability to recognize familiar faces would certainly cause people to have some sort of meaningful break with reality. How well would you do day to day if you couldn't recognize anyone you knew? Perhaps such a disease would make Holden happier as he could use it as an excuse for other behavior. However, unlike depression, prosopagnosia is not treatable with counseling or medication. While the cause of prosopagnosia is not well understood, it is thought that there is some damage to the occipitotemporal lobes of the brain.

There are important differences and similarities between these two examples of mental disorder. Depression and prosopagnosia both require that the clinician look at the person's particular behavior and ask her about her own awareness of her mental life (how it feels or seems to her at times) and then match the behavior and introspectionist reports (reports of a person on how certain things feel or seem to him or her) against specific criteria. Typically we find such criteria listed in a manual like *Diagnostic and Statistical Manual of Mental Disorders*, or DSM for short. If we find that the behavior

---

[1] *The Man Who Mistook His Wife for a Hat,* Harper, 1985.

matches a particular set of symptoms in the DSM, we can conclude that the person is suffering from a particular disorder. In both cases we needs a trained clinician to diagnose the problem and there are treatments which attempt to deal with the condition. Were Holden to be examined by a trained clinician, it's possible that he could be diagnosed with a mental disorder such as depression or manic depression. While depression and prosopagnosia both have similarities relative to diagnosis, there are some important differences that highlight issues with mental disorder in general.

What's different between the two conditions is that depression, given all the recent research, does not have an obvious physical cause. While the cause of prosopagnosia is not exactly known, it's generally thought that there is some problem with the occipitotemporal lobes of the brain. But with depression there's no real distinct neural cause that researchers agree upon. There's certainly an imbalance of neurochemicals in the brain that has been recently linked to depression and treatment regimens focus on restoring proper balance. But treatment of depression with drugs will not completely cure the condition. Even when the disordered brain states are realigned and made normal through drug treatment, depression can often remain. Counseling is often required to further restore the person to the non-depressed state. And often counseling will reveal that there has been some sort of traumatic event the person has witnessed or experienced (like Holden's witnessing of a suicide or the death of his brother) that will be the trigger for depression.

Depression and its treatment are then different from the case of prosopagnosia. There is no medication or counseling that will fix this disorder. And this comes from the understood cause of the condition: a neural problem. There is some loss of neural function that then causes the person to be unable to recognize faces. In general, there is no psychological trauma that precedes prosopagnosia, but there is often some sort of neural damage like a stroke or head injury. This is similar to when a person loses the ability to speak as a result of a stroke. The cause of the issue isn't psychological, as is often the case with depression, but is neuro-physical.

This distinction in causes of disorder (or etiology as it is known in the clinical world) shows an important issue with regard to mental disorder and its diagnosis. It's often difficult to tell if certain people have a mental disorder. Some years ago, the diagnosis of mental disorders was thought to be too variable. Since many of the mental conditions lacked any discernible physical basis, a push was made to codify the diagnostic criteria (this gave rise to manuals like the DSM) and then attempts to find the physical basis of disorders.

This push towards medicalization is a direct result of trying to deal with two problems to which the concept of mental disorder gives rise. The first is the ambiguity found in the behavior-based criteria in the manuals used to diagnose a disorder. Depression has a number of behavioral criteria associated with it, but many can be vague and could apply to all of us at one time or another. The main behavioral indicators of depression are depressed mood, feeling sad or empty and periods of listlessness or low energy.

Holden's behavior could count as depressed behavior in one regard or another. All of us have exhibited some or all of those criteria. In other disorders the criteria for diagnosis will often be some comparison with a normal group or normal pattern. In autism, some of the criteria for diagnosis are failure to develop language or normal peer relationships by a certain age. But as many of us know, children often develop skills at different rates, so the criteria can be difficult to apply. There has to be some sustained levels of these conditions over time in the case of depression, and there are other criteria that need to be met to form a complete diagnosis, so the fact that we all have felt some of the states associated with depression at one time or another, or that certain children do develop at differing rates doesn't invalidate the use of the criterion as a proper diagnostic tool.

The second problem—related to the first, but more focused on the use and vagueness of certain criteria—focuses on when something rises to the level of meaningful break with reality, or a violation of normal patterns of behavior. A person in one case could violate normal patterns according to one group and not be considered abnormal by another. And this case can be exemplified by looking more closely at Holden Caulfield.

Holden's Crumby Mental Disorder

Holden, as we can tell early on, is a troubled kid. He's in his fourth high school and is awaiting the official notification of his expulsion and the impending fall-out from his family. He seems to say things that are obvious exaggerations, he's irritable, is set off by things he doesn't even believe should set him off (his roommate's back-seat excursion with a girl whom he knows), and puts himself into dangerous positions. He drinks when he shouldn't, treks through New York City late into the evening, spends his own Christmas money on women and wine, and takes his sister's money. And of course there is his near brush with death as he wildly walks the streets of New York City while conversing with his dead brother.

All this and more can reasonably lead us to believe that there's something wrong with Holden. And it seems that there is hardly reason not to suspect that Holden does suffer from some sort of mental disorder like manic depression. But aside from the last mentioned behavior of his walking through the streets and nearly getting killed, the behavior he exhibits might not be all that different from that of a typical teenage boy. Most teenagers behave in suspect fashion. Most teenagers can be set off by seemingly innocuous events. Most teenagers will avoid their parents at times. Indeed, if the near-death walk through the streets was an isolated event that never occurred again, would we really be strongly committed to calling a teenager acting in the way Holden does mentally disordered? The case that Holden presents is woefully underdetermined relative to a diagnosis, but more than that, the criteria themselves may not solve the ambiguity issue.

Imagine an adult behaving like Holden. It may turn out to be a whole lot easier to diagnose an adult with these behaviors as suffering from a mental disorder than Holden, especially if that adult had a standard nine-to-five job with a family and sufficiently complex social life. If teenagers are expected (in our culture) to be irrational, irritable, and prone to mood swings, then such behaviors are normal and are not indicative of a mental disorder. If adults are not expected to behave in such ways, then maybe we would diagnose them as suffering a mental disorder because such behavior would cause them to have meaningful breaks with their family, social, and working life. The important point here is that the class against which the subject is evaluated in order to make the discovery that they are not acting normally is crucially important.

There's another problem with applying to Holden the crite-ria for a mental disorder. Remember that we have only a couple days of exposure to Holden and his behavior. He's about to be expelled from his fourth high school and this indicates a trou-bled past, but there's nothing by itself in that fact to indicate that he suffers from a mental disorder. When he was expelled from his first school, it might have been very near to the death of his brother. It wouldn't be hard to believe that he was just having a hard time adjusting to the loss of his brother and was acting out.

Parents and administrators may agree that a change of scenery is just what's needed. Perhaps the second school is the one where he witnessed the suicide of a classmate. Such a trau-matic experience could cause any one to leave. As for the third school, he may just not have fit in very well. Regardless of the order in which any of the events are related to the later expul-sions, these can all be explained as typical reactions of a teenage boy. Not that they are the best ways to deal with the issues, but they are certainly not ones that would make us assume Holden necessarily suffers from a mental disorder.

But in the book, we catch Holden at his nadir. He's getting kicked out of another school; he's unmotivated and appears to be just giving up— typical behavior for a youth. Add to this the non-chalance with which Holden ends the story. He seems confused, but mostly he seems irritated, not overly so, but just the irrita-tion of someone who wants to get on with the day. What this sug-gests is that we can't be sure if Holden's behavior indicates a mental disorder. The criteria for depression may be met, but they are worded in such a way that a great many behaviors may qual-ify and yet the person they apply to may not be depressed.

We need a whole lot more information. We would want to know if depression ran in the family—genetic predisposition. Has the behavior just manifested itself or has he always been this way? What are his friends' and teachers' opinions? Without this additional information we simply can't make a medical diagnosis of Holden. All that said, there is something disturb-ing about Holden and the way he behaves that causes us to wonder if all is as it should be in his mental life. He's particu-larly crumby to a lot of people—even ones he loves.

But perhaps the example of Holden Caulfield is not enough to show the wide variability of deciding who is suffering a mental disorder and who is not. What if an adult, with no family to support, who was by and large a loner or recluse (as Salinger was), exhibited behaviors such as the ones Holden did? Would that reclusive adult think that these sorts of behaviors were symptoms of a disorder that caused a significant break with reality?

Irritability would not be an issue if he spent much time alone. If his job was such that he could work any hours he pleased and late night jaunts and irregular schedule did not affect him, then he might not even notice the behavior to be something capable of distress. Further, he may find ways to work around such issues. What if Holden were able to work around his behavior swings, graduate from high school, and make it through college or hold down a job? In the same way that a person who is red-green color-blind recognizes the green light as being the light that is lowest on the traffic signal, the person who may fit the diagnosis of "depression" might function well enough so that there would be no motivation to seek diagnosis or therapy, either counseling or drugs. The very grounds that would cause us to consult the DSM or a trained professional for a diagnosis simply evaporate. Hence no diagnosis is made or even in need of being made since the person is functioning well and is not having "meaningful" breaks with reality. This case of the ambiguity of criteria and their applicability to a wide range of cases is made even clearer when you compare cultures or generations. The ambiguity can be seen in another example of possible mental disorder: ADD/ADHD.

ADD—A Crumby Cultural Problem

The recent precipitous rise of the diagnoses of Attention Deficit Disorder (ADD) or Attention Deficit/Hyperactivity Disorder (ADHD) has been thought to be the result of a clash of rival demands that are the result of new modes of learning and behavior traceable to technology. It's thought that the behaviors coincident with a diagnosis of ADD or ADHD are the result of children coping with a world where information comes to us with great speed and there are multiple vehicles through which to get this information. Hence it's important not to focus too much on any one task.

So for people raised in a multiple-media world it pays to be able to pay attention to a multitude of things rather than focusing solely on one thing like sitting still or listening in class. These are exactly the sorts of difficulties that Holden exhibits. He couldn't keep paying attention to the lecture about the Egyptians, or keep his mind from wandering to other topics not related to the current conversation he was having, such as when he asked if one of his female friends kept all her kings on the back row.

The ability to multitask is thus a boon for a person now. So rather than creating a meaningful break with reality, ADD/ADHD is an adaptive behavior rather than one that is disordered. It's only disordered relative to a now outmoded, or unnecessary form of learning where multi-media was not as influential. There's a real worry that the diagnosis of ADD/ADHD as a mental disorder is just a particular way a society at a particular time views certain behaviors. Since our culture doesn't value such skills, we classify them as mental deficiencies and not adaptive behaviors. If the child exhibiting the behaviors we associate with ADD/ADHD were raised in a culture where such behavior is praised, it would be encouraged rather than viewed as a disorder. Thus the concept of mental disorder is fraught with non-objective factors that call into question the efficacy of the notion of mental disorder in the first place.

If Holden's frenetic behavior and racing mind were prized in a culture where information flowed at a much higher rate than his, then he might be considered healthy and even having desirable traits. If simply changing your culture would have you no longer identified as suffering a mental disorder, then in what sense is the mental disorder a real objective feature of your mental life? Seemingly none is the answer and such an answer has been offered by a number of critics of the concept of mental disorder such as Michel Foucault.

Beyond the cultural relativity issue, what the cases of depression and ADD/ADHD and the diagnosis of them also show is that the criteria used in the diagnosis of mental disorders are not easily applied in all areas. Before the diagnosis of manic depression came into fashion, a person might have been called high-strung or eccentric rather than suffering from anxiety or manic depression. Thus, the criteria of mental disorder are open to interpretation on a variety of levels—cultural, generational and personal—which presents problems for the belief that their application is objective. Objective application is crucially important if there is to be such a thing as mental disorder.

This desire for objectivity is what really drives the medicalization of the diagnosis of mental disorders. If we were able to find that mental disorders had unique neuro-physical correlates that we could use to identify a particular disorder (genetic abnormalities, neurochemical imbalances, malformed neural structures) we could abandon the use of the behavioral criteria and diagnose Holden with depression. If his brain showed abnormalities indicative of depression then he qualifies as depressed even if the behaviors don't rise to a level of a meaningful break with reality. The interpretation issues that beset the use of the ambiguous criteria could be avoided and all we would need to look for would be physical abnormalities.

However, finding neuro-physical correlates for most or all mental disorders would not guarantee objectivity or reliable diagnosis of an actual mental disorder. Again, contrasting prosopagnosia with depression helps us make the point. What leads a person to wonder whether they or another person is suffering from a mental disorder? It would obviously be some sort of loss of ability relative to a previous part of their lives. Holden never once seems to really contemplate his behavior as troubling, except maybe when he's talking with Phoebe.

In contrast, the person with prosopagnosia simply finds that they are not recognizing people they believe they should. It begins to cause problems, which is to say that it causes a meaningful break with reality. Perhaps, in the future, the technology will be available to evaluate the occipito-temporal lobes and diagnose some sort of neuro-abnormality that we know is associated with prosopagnosia. If this happens, then we can diagnose the person with a certain mental disorder. This sort of case, one that moves from a personal awareness of a problem, to seeking medical help, to a medical investigation and the final diagnosis based on an objective brain scan identifying the neuro-abnormality associated with the very behaviors associated with prosopagnosia, is textbook and comforting.

However, this sort of clean and neat series of events may not comport well with other forms of mental disorder. For the person suffering depression, he or she will notice that certain things that used to be easy to do or brought joy no longer do. Maybe they find getting up in the morning to be difficult, or maybe they have disproportionate emotional responses to events such as when Holden became so enraged at his roommate's possible sexual tryst with a former girlfriend that he got into a fight he knew he would lose. Whatever symptoms the depressive person suffers, these are only symptoms when they rise to a level where there is a disturbance in a person's daily life.

But if certain criteria of a mental disorder were not viewed by the person or the culture as particularly troubling, there would be no need to diagnose the problem as a mental disorder. Thus, there would be no further reason to look for neuro-physical correlates. Someone could then have the neuro-abnormality present, but never be in a position to have it diagnosed. While not recognizing faces may be a basic issue that many people would find troubling, depression isn't so clear-cut. It could be that the person sees herself as pessimistic rather than depressed. She may function well in her day to day life or get by.

This seems exactly what we see with Holden. Holden would not think he's had any "meaningful break with reality," and would never seek treatment or diagnosis. He's very nonchalant about the whole ordeal, after all. If a person never thinks there's a problem to begin with, there would never be a reason to seek any sort of medical evaluation to see if there was a neuro-abnormality—which is exactly what would occur for someone who could no longer recognize faces. As with Holden's refusal to see his behavior as troubling, there would be no reason to test the chemicals in the brain to see if there was an imbalance. If there is no test, then there's never a reason to look for an abnormality and there may be people who live with certain neuro-physical peculiarities who are never diagnosed and never feel the need to be diagnosed.

While we may be a bit skeptical that the case of the borderline depressives may not really threaten the practice of relying on neuro-physical markers for diagnosis (since these individuals are borderline and we mustn't draw inferences from a special group), there are yet other reasons not to rely wholly on neuro-physical markers for diagnosis of mental disorders. For example, it has been thought that one of the causes of Alzheimer's disease is the presence of plaques in the brain: a neuro-abnormality. This was taken to be diagnostic: an objective neuro-physical component of the disorder. But it was later discovered that many brains of those of advanced age had plaques and they had never had any signs of Alzheimer's.

If that's correct, there may be people who exhibit unusual neuro-physical characteristics that would make it easy to diagnose them with a certain mental disorder, but who function perfectly normally and are not borderline in any way. This calls into question the importance of the neuro-physical marker relative to the diagnosis of Alzheimer's and perhaps to any mental disorder more generally. Without these neuro-physical markers to rely on, we're left only with behaviors to use for diagnosis and as has been argued above, behaviors alone do not get us everything that we'd need to know in order to reliably diagnose a certain mental disorder.

So Is Holden's Crumbiness Really a Mentally Disorder?

Holden's behaviors may not rise to a level requiring a diagnosis of a particular disorder like depression or manic depression, but they are worrisome and it seems reasonable to have a clinician at least evaluate him. But the difficulties in understanding mental disorders mentioned above and the ambiguity of Holden's case caution us in our understanding of mental disorders in general.

Holden *was* sent to a place where one of the people who saw him was a psychoanalyst. He was sent to this place by his parents as a result of his behavior. Regardless of what sort of facility Holden was sent to, it's clear that Holden is a bit off—and this is one of the reasons he's such an interesting character. But if mental disorders have, at base, some sort of cultural component and there has been a precipitous rise in the diagnosis of certain disorders like depression, ADD/ADHD and autism, this leads us to wonder if there really are as many cases out there as the numbers seems to indicate. For example, in the United States during the 1940s mental health was not a widely discussed topic. The work of psychotherapists was largely underappreciated. Most persons didn't talk about or seek any sort of medical intervention for what we, today, would call a mental health problem. People just got through the issues.

Holden, for all his misbehaving, would have probably been placed in another school and eventually graduated or passed on. He may have been considered a problem child, or the black sheep, but more than likely if he had grown up to be moderately self-sufficient, the behavior of his younger days would have been written off as a sort of youthful indiscretion or rebellion; most certainly not a form of mental disorder.

But given the modern United States and our state boards of mental health and the prevalence of therapy or rehab, Holden would be much more likely to be diagnosed with some sort of mental disorder such as depression, or manic-depression and then be given a course of treatments ranging from therapy to pharmaceutical intervention. In a mere sixty years the same behaviors have gone from troublesome but of little worry to ones in need of medical intervention. This seems to be a problem for mental disorders as an idea.

There is a cultural element to this change. It was the culture that started to recognize these behaviors as more than eccentricities. It was the culture that took mental health seriously. While there may yet be some basic problem about mental health that any diagnosis detects, it may not be something that we would pay attention to were it not for the fact that we have the concept of mental disorder in our vocabulary.

If this chapter is convincing, then we will find the drastic rise in such mental disorders to be more reflective of social change rather than an actual increase in the numbers of real disorders and Holden would, in modern times, be likely headed to some sort of mental health treatment program. What contributes more to the rise in cases is that clinicians and the society overall are over-diagnosing the problem—being far too inclusive of what sorts of behaviors should be considered in the diagnosis of depression.

And so we arrive at the conclusion that Holden may or may not be depressed. We have a limited pool of evidence, ambiguities in the story, and a general worry about the aptness of mental disorders overall. In a world in which healthcare and mental health are increasingly important topics both politically and personally, it's important to understand the issues surrounding the idea of a mental disorder and what having one or being diagnosed with one may in fact mean.

16
Calling Salinger Up

KEITH DROMM and HEATHER SALTER

The philosopher Noël Carroll says that reading a book is like being a participant in a conversation.[1] Holden tells us that after reading a good book, he'd like nothing more than to be able to talk with its author:

> What really knocks me out is a book that, when you're all done reading it, you wish the author that wrote it was a terrific friend of yours and you could call him up on the phone whenever you felt like it. (3, p. 25)

But if any fans of Salinger had tried to call him up, they would at best have reached a secretary, an editor, or an assistant. From 1953 till his death in 2010, Salinger was the most famous and mythologized recluse in literary history. Although he had friends, went on vacations with his family, and went shopping once a week in Windsor, Vermont, Salinger generally refused to answer questions about his writing. Among the topics that fans could have discussed with Salinger were the meanings of parts or the entirety of *The Catcher in the Rye*. But since no one could ever just "call him up" and have their questions about the novel's meaning answered, how well can we understand *The Catcher in the Rye*?

Fans of *Catcher* felt the same way about Salinger that Holden feels about his favorite authors, but their preferred

---

[1] Noël Carroll, "Art, Intention, and Conversation," in Gary Iseminger, editor, *Intention and Interpretation*, Temple University Press, 1992.

form of contact was the mail. Although his fans predicted Salinger probably would not answer their letters, many of them wrote anyway in the hope that he would honor them with a reply. While working as an assistant to Salinger's agent at Harold Ober Associates, Joanna Smith Rakoff had the job of answering Salinger's fan mail, which came from all over the world: Denmark, Japan, Sri Lanka, and so on. A recurring theme that Rakoff discovered in the letters was fans saying that Holden Caulfield was the literary character most like them. Rakoff believes that Salinger's fans responded to the sincerity in his writing. They connected with Holden because they, too, were misfits surrounded by phonies. Since they believed that Salinger had molded Holden after himself, they connected with Salinger as well and wanted to be friends with him. In one letter, a man from North Carolina, writes, "I'd get one helluva kick outta you if you wrote back and told me I was a bastard!"[2] In their letters, many fans confess that *Catcher* is the only book they have ever liked. A freshman high-school girl writes that the only book she ever loved is *The Catcher in the Rye* and if Salinger were to write her back her English teacher will change her failing grade to an "A" (p. 316). The letter that stands out to Rakoff the most is from a boy in Atlanta. He writes:

> I think about Holden a lot. He just pops into my mind's eye and I get to thinking about him dancing with old Phoebe or horsing around at the bathroom mirror at Pencey. When I first think about him I usually get a big stupid grin on my face. You know thinking about what a funny guy he is and all. But then, I usually get depressed as hell. I guess I get depressed because I only think about Holden when I'm feeling very emotional. I can get quite emotional. Don't worry though. I've learned that, as phony as it may be, you can't go around revealing your goddamn emotions to the world. (p. 324)

In this letter, as in many others, the fan tries to adopt Holden's speech and believes that he can confide in Salinger as a trusted friend. He also praises the universal and relatable qualities in Salinger's characters.

---

[2] Joanna Smith Rakoff, "My Salinger Year," in Catherine Crawford, editor, *If You Really Want to Hear about It*, Thunder's Mouth, 2006, p. 313.

In addition to expressing admiration, a letter or a phone call to the author might elicit answers to questions about a work's meaning. Of course, we don't have to call the author up for these. Many authors give interviews or write essays in which they discuss their work. They might not answer all of our questions, but there are often other ways of getting them answered. We can read biographies about the author and other accounts of his or her life, or other works by the author. The information we gather from these sources can help us answer questions about the novel. For example, knowing something about the author's religious beliefs might help us to understand his or her novel. If we know that the author is Christian, then we know that she perhaps believes in redemption for her characters. We know that Salinger followed the teachings of various Eastern religion and even Scientology at different points of his life, but there's a lot we don't know about Salinger, such as whether or not *Catcher* was autobiographical. Salinger didn't answer fan mail, and he wasn't the type of author you could just call up.

When a journalist did manage to pin him down, Salinger despised more than any other inquiry the question about whether *Catcher* was autobiographical, and in three separate interviews, he answers the question differently. In 1953, before his seclusion and complete distrust of journalists, Salinger granted an interview to Shirlie Blaney. In the interview, he is cooperative and generous. When she asks him whether *Catcher* was autobiographical, he says, "Sort of, I was much relieved when I finished it. My boyhood was very much the same as that of the boy in the book, and it was a great relief telling people about it."[3] Then much later, Salinger tells Michael Clarkson in 1979, "There's absolutely no autobiography in my stories."[4] A few years after his interview with Clarkson, in a 1980 interview with Betty Eppes, Salinger refuses to answer questions about *Catcher*, and when she asks the same question Blaney and Clarkson had posed in their interviews, he says that he doesn't know anymore whether or not Holden is autobiographical.[5]

---

[3] Shirlie Blaney, "Interview with J.D. Salinger," in Crawford, p. 4.

[4] Michael Clarkson "'Catching the 'Catcher in the Rye' J.D. Salinger," *If You Really Want to Hear about It*, p. 51.

[5] Betty Eppes, "What I Did Last Summer," *If You Really Want to Hear about It*, p. 35.

As fans, we may feel as if Salinger's reticence about his work has left us in the dark about what he intended the novel and its various elements to mean. Why is Holden so obsessed with the ducks in Central Park, why doesn't he have sex with Sunny, is he mentally ill, is *he* a phony, and so on? Maybe we could figure these things out on our own, but if he answered when we called, Salinger could have filled us in on his intentions behind these and other elements of his novel. However, some philosophers hold that an author's intentions don't matter to our understanding of his or her work. What he or she intended to mean makes no difference to how we should interpret the work. Others hold that the author's intentions matter most of all. What the author intended should determine how we interpret the work. Still others contend that only the intentions of "hypothetical" authors should guide our interpretations.

Hang Up That Phone!

The view that author's intentions don't matter to our questions about a novel's meaning was once very popular in the field of literary criticism and still is to some extent. This is known as the *anti-intentionalist* position. In 1946, William Wimsatt, Jr. and Monroe C. Beardsley wrote a very influential essay defending this view titled "The Intentional Fallacy."[6] The fallacy referred to in the title is committed when we consult the author's biography or other evidence of his or her intentions in order to figure out the meaning of his or her writing. Wimsatt and Beardsley argue that such evidence is unnecessary for our interpretations. Either the author succeeded in her intentions or she failed. If she succeeded, then there is no need to consult external evidence to get at the text's meaning; it's contained in the text. If the author failed in her intention, then the intended meaning is not in the text. If we call the author up and she tells us what meaning she intended to put there, that won't change the fact that it's not there. If we go ahead and read the text with that meaning, we are reading that meaning *into* the text.

---

[6] Reprinted in many places, including *Praising it New: The Best of New Criticism*, edited by Garrick Davis, Swallow Press/University of Ohio Press, 2008.

The views of Beardsley and Wimsatt had a hand in creating New Criticism. Others who influenced New Criticism include T.S. Eliot, Ezra Pound, and I. A. Richards. In addition to Beardsley and Wimsatt, creators of New Criticism also include the following poets, all born between 1888 and 1907: Robert Penn Warren, Cleanth Brooks, Yvor Winters, and Kenneth Burke.[7] New Criticism maintains that determining the aesthetic value of a poem or novel is more important than discovering facts about the author's life. William Logan states: "New Criticism takes as its task to understand how meaning and feeling are invented in language... and to judge if some poems are better than others...in aesthetic terms" (p. xiv). The words on the page are all that matter to New Critics. Biographical details about the author are irrelevant.

Though he never said so directly, Salinger might have liked New Criticism since he detested journalists and critics peeking into his life. He preferred to live in secret and seclusion, and he even became angry with his children when they revealed details about their family, as revealed throughout his daughter Margaret's memoir *Dream Catcher*. In the introduction of her memoir, Margaret Salinger states, "I was nearly middle aged before I broke the silence, broke the family idol guarding generations of moldy secrets both real and imagined, and began to shed some light and fresh air, wholesome and life-giving as Cornish breeze."[8] Perhaps Salinger shared the belief of the New Critics that being too concerned with the author leads to critics "truffle-hunting the sins"[9] of the author when the focus should be on appreciating the aesthetic value of the novel. The implication of this view is that when interpreting literary works, interviewing the author is unnecessary. This is another point with which Salinger might have agreed. When Betty Eppes asked Salinger questions about Holden Caulfield, specifically if Holden ever grows up, Salinger's advice to Eppes was to "Read the book. It's all in the book. There's no more to

---

[7] William Logan, "Forward into the Past: Reading the New Critics," *Praising It New*, pp. xi–xii.

[8] Margaret A. Salinger, *Dream Catcher: A Memoir*, Simon and Schuster, 2000, p. xiii.

[9] "Forward into the Past," p. xv.

Holden Caulfield." Salinger felt that there was no need to ask him questions about his intentions or about his life.

Go Ahead and Call

There's something correct about Salinger's remark that "It's all in the book." If an author entirely failed in conveying what he or she meant, no amount of external evidence is going to change that. Consider slips of the tongue; maybe the person who makes one meant to say something else, but she still made the slip and instead said something that has a different meaning or no meaning at all. Their original intentions cannot change that fact. However, it is rarely failures like this that prompt us to consult an author's biography or call him or her up on the phone. More often the meaning of the text is unclear, not entirely absent from it. This typically happens when a sentence, passage, or motif is ambiguous or in some other way allows for more than one interpretation. In such cases, it seems that the best way to resolve the ambiguity is simply asking the author what he or she meant, and if that's not possible, then determining his or her intention in some other way.

To help us see how this is true, we can distinguish between three types of meaning for a sentence, such as the one Holden utters when Ackley asks him if the book he's reading is any good: "This *sen*tence I'm reading is terrific" (3, p. 28). Holden's sentence has a *sentence meaning*, a *speaker's meaning*, and *word sequence meaning*.[10] Sentence meaning is the meaning that this particular sequence of words has when it used by Holden in response to Ackley's question. This meaning is the target of our interpretative efforts. Speaker's meaning is the meaning that Holden intends to convey by using that sequence of words. The word sequence meaning is the meaning that collection of words has outside of any particular use of them.

These words can be used by different speakers to mean different things. When Holden says them to Ackley, he is being sarcastic; as he explains, "I can be quite sarcastic when I'm in the mood" (3, p. 28). So, he doesn't really mean that the sen-

---

[10] See William Tolhurst, "On What a Text Is and What It Means," *British Journal of Aesthetics* 19.

tence he's reading is terrific (word sequence meaning). He does-n't really enjoy reading this sentence over and over again, and he's hoping that Ackley will understand what he actually means and leave him alone so he can read the rest of the sentences in the book. Someone *could* use those very same words to mean that the sentence is terrific. In that case the sentence meaning would be the same as the word sequence meaning. What makes the difference in the two cases is the speaker's intention; it is only by knowing that intention (or the speaker's meaning) that we can understand the sentence meaning of "This sentence I'm reading is terrific."

Ackley thinks Holden is being sincere, as Holden points out: "He didn't get it though" (3, p. 28). If Ackley had instead been unsure whether Holden was being sarcastic, he could have asked him something like, "Are you being serious?" He'd be asking for Holden's intentions in saying those words. Holden could have then pointed out to him that he intended to be sarcastic. In understanding his use of those words (the sentence meaning), Holden's intentions matter. They determine whether the sentence should be taken sarcastically, for its more typical word sequence meaning, or for some other possible meaning. So, anti-intentionalists are wrong if they believe that word sequence meaning alone is all we need to interpret a text. We also need to know the speaker's reasons for using those words, in other words, his or her intentions.

The view that author's intentions matter to our interpretations of what they write is known as *actual intentionalism* (the reason for "actual" will become clear eventually). E.D. Hirsch is an important advocate of actual intentionalism. He writes that "meaning is an affair of consciousness not of words." [11] He believes that words only acquire a definite meaning when there is an intention behind their use.

To illustrate this point, imagine that the first astronauts to land on the surface of Mars discover an interesting rock. Because of erosion and some other events in its creation, there are a set of unusual marks on its otherwise smooth surface. These marks look exactly like this: THIS SENTENCE THAT I'M READING IS TERRIFIC. They resemble the sentence (as

---

[11] E.D. Hirsch, "In Defense of the Author," in Iseminger, *Intention and Interpretation*, Temple University Press, 1992, p. 16.

written) that Holden uttered to Ackley. The astronauts know, however, that no one inscribed those marks into the rock. They were formed through entirely natural processes. Now, the very same marks can be used by someone to convey a meaning. An astronaut who wants one of his colleagues to stop bothering him while he's trying to read a book could pick up the rock and show it to him when he's asked by his annoying colleague whether it's any good. However, without a consciousness behind either their creation or use, those marks are meaningless. We might say they have word sequence meaning, but that only means that they could be used meaningfully by someone to express a thought. Hirsch is correct that without someone intending to use them in such a way, they are a not meaningful sequence of words (the marks on the rock aren't even words).

However, consciousness does not always or fully determine meaning; in other words, speaker's meaning is not always identical to sentence meaning. In cases of slips of the tongue or malapropisms, what is said was not intended by the speaker. In such cases, we typically absolve the speaker of the word sequence meaning. That is, we don't attribute any meaning those words might have to the speaker (although we sometimes take a slip of the tongue to be what we call "Freudian," so as unintentionally revealing something about the person who makes it). We don't, however, simply invest the sequence of words with the intended meaning. People cannot mean whatever they want by the words they use.

If Holden says to a bartender "Give me a Tom Collins," he can't complain when he gets served a Tom Collins instead of the scotch and soda that he intended to order. He might have committed a slip of the tongue, but that doesn't change the meanings of the words he utters. His intentions or anything else going on in his consciousness cannot make "Tom Collins" mean scotch and soda.

Because our intentions do not have the power to change the meanings of words, Noël Carroll and some other philosophers endorse what is called *moderate actual intentionalism.* This theory of interpretation "only claims that the artist's actual intentions are relevant to interpretation"; our interpretations are "constrained" by those intentions but those intentions don't fully determine the meaning of a literary work.[12] So, authors cannot mean *whatever* they want by what they write. What those words can possibly mean is restricted by the rules of syntax and semantics. As Carroll explains, moderate actual intentionalism holds that "the author's intention must square with what he has written, but if it squares with what he has written, then the author's intention is authoritative" (77). According to Carroll's theory, Holden, as the author of that sentence he utters to Ackley, has final say over its meaning as long as his intended meaning is compatible with—or can be expressed by—those words. Similarly, Salinger is the authority over the meaning of *Catcher*, but it must be possible for *Catcher* to convey the meaning he intends for it.

When the speaker's meaning is incompatible with word sequence meaning—in other words, when those words just cannot be used to convey the intended meaning—then we simply don't have a sentence; instead, as philosopher Gary Iseminger puts it, we have a "failure or a (nonverbal) joke of some sort."[13] Such a sentence would be like the one found on the Martian rock. In these cases there is no problem with interpretation; we shouldn't even try to understand such a sentence.

Just Pretend to Call the Author Up

Intentions certainly matter in our interpretations of the words of others. Holden couldn't get out of his poor performance on his history exam by interpreting Mr. Spencer's instructions to mean that the essay should provide as little information as possible on the Egyptians while fulfilling the length requirements (2, p. 16). No matter how viable his interpretation is according to the standards of New Criticism, Mr. Spencer's intentions—as long as they are compatible with the words he wrote—determine the *correct* interpretation. In fact, as we have seen, without those intentions the words would have no meaning.

However, some philosophers hold that while intentions do matter, the intentions of the *actual* author of the text do not.

---

[12] Noël Carroll, "Interpretation and Intention: The Debate between Hypothetical and Actual Intentionalism," *Metaphilosophy* 31 (January 2000), p. 76.

[13] Gary Iseminger, "Actual Intentionalism vs. Hypothetical Intentionalism," *Journal of Aesthetics and Art Criticism* 54 (1996), p. 322.

This is because novels, like other kinds of literature and every other sort of artwork, are different than history exam instructions, as well as such things as drink orders or sarcastic remarks. Unlike these other uses of words, novels are autonomous from their authors. When they publish their works, authors give them over to the public. They become more important than the intentions of the author. The anti-intentionalists Wimsatt and Beardsley hold a similar view about literary works; they say that once a literary work is published "it is detached from the author . . . and goes about the world beyond his power to intend about it or control it. . . . it belongs to the public" (pp. 104–05). A drink order remains the possession of its author; for example, he has the power to change it. A novel becomes public property once it's published; the author can't take it back.

This approach to interpreting novels and other artworks is known as *hypothetical intentionalism*. It holds that we should only appeal to the intentions of a hypothetical or postulated author when interpreting a literary work. This permits us to draw upon what we know about the actual author's time period and culture, but evidence from the author's biography, even statements by the author about his or her intentions, should not be consulted. As Jerold Levinson puts it, reading should not be a matter of "detective investigation" or "biographical sleuthing."[14] This is another way that hypothetical intentionalists are like anti-intentionalists, such as the New Critics. They differ from them, however, in recognizing that meaning cannot be entirely divorced from intention. But the hypothetical intentionalists don't think we need biographies or phone calls to arrive at these intentions. All we need are hypotheses about intentions that are based on general facts about the composition of the novel.

It may happen that when we follow this approach we arrive at two or more equally viable hypotheses. They are all compatible with the text and the evidence we're permitted to consult. Many hypothetical intentionalists tell us that when this occurs, we should prefer the aesthetically superior interpreta-

---

[14] Jerold Levinson, "Hypothetical Intentionalism: Statement, Objections, and Replies," in Michael Krausz, editor, *Is There a Single Right Interpretation?*, Penn State University Press, 2002), p. 315.

tion. They believe that we should read the work according to this interpretation even if it is incompatible with an aesthetically inferior meaning intended by the actual author.[15] Imagine we had managed to get Salinger on the phone and he told us the meaning of *The Catcher of the Rye*, but this is what he said: "It is a warning against underage drinking and dropping out of school. Holden is a spoiled rich kid who should be put into reformatory school. He doesn't need psychiatric help; he needs a good kick in the ass ... and a job." This *meaning* of *Catcher* would conflict with those that most fans of the novel have attributed to it. It is also aesthetically inferior to those interpretations. The hypothetical intentionalists would endorse the aesthetically superior interpretation over the one Salinger gives to his own novel. The former, according to them, would be the meaning of the work.

While hypothetical intentionalism would require us to ignore the author's own intentions in favor of the aesthetically superior ones of a hypothetical author, it does so for the sake of a more satisfying experience. That, it could be argued, is the point of reading a novel. It is not to learn about the author but to have an aesthetic experience. Perhaps if we were the author's psychologist or friend we would read his novel in order to learn something about the author, but the typical readers of a novel are not reading in order to learn about the author. They want to read a *good* book, and if it takes ignoring the intentions of the book's author to do so, then they should.

You Can Call but He's Not Going to Pick Up

When we read a novel, we usually engage in hypothetical reasoning about the author's intentions. We don't have the author on the phone guiding us through his novel. We use what we know about the author's time period and culture, as well as some facts we might know about his biography, in order to interpret the words we are reading. In many cases, these are all we need to understand a text. Literary texts—given such things as their complexity, the density of their meanings, as

---

[15] This does happen. Stephen Davies gives two good examples of this happening with two literary works, in his *The Philosophy of Art*, Blackwell, 2006, pp. 120–22.

well as the preference of their authors for aesthetics over clarity—often require more interpretative work than other sorts of texts. They often leave us with questions about their meanings. To answer them, we form hypotheses that draw upon the most immediately available evidence, and we tend to prefer hypotheses that provide aesthetic satisfaction.

However, Noël Carroll points out that we can have interests other than aesthetic satisfaction that we try to satisfy when reading a novel. Carroll writes: "When we read a literary text . . . we enter a relationship with its creator that is roughly analogous to a conversation" (p. 117). Although the conversation is one-sided, reading is like other conversations in that we are aiming at understanding the other participant in it: "A fulfilling conversation requires that we have the conviction of having grasped what our interlocutor meant or intended to say" (p. 118). Carroll believes that this *conversational interest* outweighs our interest in aesthetic satisfaction: "A conversation that left us with only our own clever construals or educated guesses, no matter how aesthetically rich, would leave us with the sense that something was missing" (p. 118). In ordinary conversations, the person we were talking to would have the same impression that "something was missing" if we made no effort to understand what he or she meant by his or her words.

Authors of novels are typically trying to express something specific to their audience. Readers also often act as if they are participants in a conversation. The efforts of fans of *Catcher* to contact Salinger are evidence of this. Holden seems to regard reading a novel as like having a conversation with the author, one that he'd like to continue on the phone. These efforts to understand the author are not "biographical sleuthing." Like conversations with other strangers, we are interested only in what the author means by the words he or she is sharing with us, not his or her entire life story. However, information from an author's biography can sometimes help us understand the meanings of the words they put into a novel.

Another problem we see with both the hypothetical and anti-intentionalist approaches to interpretation is that not only do they disregard the intentions of the actual author, they disregard the text. While the typical New Critic or hypothetical intentionalist does not recognize this, their position would allow them—maybe even require them—to make alterations to the text in order to serve their purpose in reading. If that purpose is aesthetic satisfaction, then re-writing the text in order to provide that satisfaction seems perfectly permissible. Only respect for the author's intentions would require us to refrain from altering his or her text. If we are indifferent to what the author intended to write, then there's nothing stopping us from "improving" what the author wrote. So, if we were anti-intentionalists, and we believed that *Catcher* would be better with some gunfights and car chases, we should re-write the novel to put in those elements.

It's not a common practice to re-write other people's literary works. Even New Critics refrained from doing this; they tried to interpret texts as they were given to them. It is certainly something that Salinger would not have permitted. He was famously controlling over *The Catcher in the Rye*. He never sold the movie rights. Also, when Fredrik Colting published *60 Years Later: Coming Through the Rye* in 2009, a "sequel" to *Catcher* that he authored, Salinger successfully sued to stop its publication in the United States. Colting's novel tells the story of a seventy-six-year-old "Mr. C" who escapes from a nursing home and takes a journey through New York City that ends at a carrousel in Central Park. Salinger obviously felt that Holden's story was his own and he didn't want anyone else "completing" it for him. While we quoted some things said by Salinger that suggest his support of anti-intentionalism, Salinger's actions indicate that the integrity of the text was important to him and that his intentions with respect to the text were important as well.

Despite his reticence over the meaning of *Catcher*, Salinger thought *his* meaning was important. Many of his fans believed this also, otherwise they wouldn't have put so much effort into trying to learn about and contact him. While he never answered the phone when we called, there are good reasons for believing that there were some specific things that he wanted to communicate to us with his novel. If we disregard any author's intentions, we disregard an important reason for writing and reading: to be understood by and understand those we can't just call up on the phone.

Since we couldn't call Salinger up, we have to rely on hypothetical reasoning to understand much of his novel. In doing so, we needn't restrict the information we draw upon to merely the words on the page or general information about his culture and time period. We can use facts about Salinger provided by others like his daughter Margaret in her memoir. Perhaps his reticence about his work will make these questions more difficult to answer and the answers we arrive at more speculative. Yet, part of the joy of reading are these challenges. Perhaps Holden is expressing this when he tells us that a good book makes him want to call its author up to talk. Since our phone calls were never answered—and never will be now—readers of *Catcher* will have to have this conversation among themselves, as they have been doing for sixty years. They haven't tired of this conversation yet.[16]

---

[16] We thank Sarah McFarland, Pamela Francis, George Reisch, and Thomas Reynolds for comments on earlier drafts.

Phonies, Bastards, Morons, and Madmen

These are all the characters explicitly classified by Holden as phonies, bastards, morons, or madmen.

PHONIES
- Mr. Thurmer
- Mr. Ossenburger
- Ward Stradlater
- Mr. Haas
- George something
- Ernie
- Lillian Simmons
- Commander Blop
- the Disciples
- Sally Hayes
- Anne Louise Sherman
- Lieutenant Henry
- Holden

BASTARDS
- Ward Stradlater
- some monks
- Ernest Morrow
- Al Pike
- Mr. Haas
- George something
- Mr. Ossenburger
- Holden

MORONS
- Ward Stradlater
- Bernice Crabs or Krebs
- Maurice
- Holden

MADMEN
- Legion
- Holden

Goddam Hot-Shots

NIC BOMMARITO is a doctoral student in philosophy at Brown University. He writes papers in ethics, moral psychology, and Asian philosophy for five bucks a throw, fifteen the whole night. Everything he has is bourgeois as hell.

CLAUDIA FRANZISKA BRÜHWILER is a phony contributor to this book, since she's not a philosopher at all. Instead, she holds a PhD in political science from the University of St. Gallen, Switzerland, and focuses in her research on the interplay of politics and literature. She's currently working on her post-doctoral project on the reception of Ayn Rand's thought in Europe, and ultimately hopes to become a writer people like Holden would want to be friends with.

STIJN DE CAUWER obtained master's degrees in clinical psychology, philosophy, and cultural anthropology from the Universities of Gent and Leuven in Belgium. In 2012 he took Mr. Antolini's advice to apply himself and finished a PhD on Robert Musil at the University of Utrecht in the Netherlands. From the fall of 2012 he has been a post-doctoral researcher at the University of Leuven.

MICHAEL K. CUNDALL JR. is not a philosopher but he plays one on TV. He is a crazy sonuvabitch who sometimes writes on philosophy of psychology and humor and is the director of an honors program at North Carolina A&T. When not lying to people in his bio he teaches and does some other crumby things like Aikido and woodworking: honestly, he does.

KEITH DROMM is Associate Professor of Philosophy in the Louisiana Scholars' College at Northwestern State University. He's written *Sexual Harassment: An Introduction to the Conceptual and Ethical Issues* (2012), *Wittgenstein on Rules and Nature* (2008), some articles in philosophy journals, and chapters for such volumes as *The Philosophy of the X-Files, Spielberg and Philosophy,* and *The Office and Philosophy.* After publishing these things he lived for a while as a recluse like Salinger, but he stopped after he realized no one even noticed.

DON FALLIS is Professor of Information Resources and Adjunct Professor of Philosophy at the University of Arizona. He has written several philosophy articles on lying and deception, including "What Is Lying?" in the *Journal of Philosophy* and "The Mendacity Bifurcation," in *The Big Bang Theory and Philosophy.* Even so, he does not tell lies all that often. However, he is like Holden in being somewhat uncomfortable in the social world. And he too has spent quite a bit of time wandering around New York City in search of drinks.

DALE JACQUETTE is Senior Professorial Chair in Logic and Theoretical Philosophy at the University of Bern, Switzerland. He is actually not too crazy about writing these kinds of biographical statements concerning himself, if you want to know the truth. He has written other articles for popular culture and philosophy series, and even edited one of those jobs himself for another press. Articles on zombies, Satan Lord of Darkness in South Park cosmology, beer, and that kind of thing. Mostly, no kidding, he writes about philosophical logic, analytic metaphysics, including ontology, identity, and philosophy of mind, and selected figures in the history of philosophy. But don't get the wrong idea. He's not a flit or a duff or anything, even if he always has a squeezer of Vicks Nasal Drops on his desk.

RUSSELL MANNING teaches Philosophy at Yarra Valley Grammar in Melbourne, Australia. He applied for and was rejected by Pencey Prep.

RICK MAYOCK is still wondering where the ducks go when the lagoon gets all icy and frozen over. He can shoot the old bull with you and think about those ducks at the same time. He teaches philosophy at West Los Angeles College and is a frequent contributor to philosophy and popular culture volumes, including *The Beatles and Philosophy, The Office and Philosophy, Alice in Wonderland and Philosophy, The Rolling Stones and Philosophy: It's Just a Thought Away,* and *Jeopardy! and Philosophy: What Is Knowledge in the Form of a Question?.*

ELIZABETH OLSON lives in Minneapolis and works in the finance arena, moonlighting as a writer and cellist in her spare time. After being told by countless people that one must read *The Catcher in the Rye* as a teenaged boy or not at all, she picked up the book (as a close-to-middle aged woman) and found she loved it. (Take that, teenaged boys . . .)

GUY PINKU received his MA in cognitive psychology from Ben-Gurion University and his PhD in philosophy from the University of Haifa, Israel. Pinku went on to post-doctoral work at Washington University of St. Louis and at the University of Central Florida. *The Catcher in the Rye* is one of his favorites; in his youth he read it many times and used to know parts of it by heart. He feels that, in a sense, this book, years ago, saved his life.

HEATHER SALTER is an English instructor at Northwestern State University of Louisiana. She has written essays for the *Dictionary of Literary Biography* and *Louisiana Folklife*. Her essay about culinary symbolism in Sandra Cisneros's *Caramelo* will appear in the upcoming collection *Boarderlands: Food, Language, and the Postnation in Chicano/a Literature*. And that's all she's going to tell about. She could probably tell you more and what she plans to do next and all, but she doesn't feel like it.

MARCUS SCHULZKE is an ABD PhD candidate in political science at the University at Albany. His research interests include contemporary political theory, applied ethical theory, military ethics, video games, and comparative politics. He has published journal articles and book chapters on each of these subjects. His dissertation is a study of how soldiers think about the ethical problems that arise in combat. During his free time, Marcus studies mummies and hopes that someday modern science will be able to discover the secret ingredients that prevent them from rotting.

DONNA MARIE SMITH is a librarian at the Palm Beach County Library System which celebrates the "freedom to read," including reading all of J.D. Salinger's books. She's been involved in several projects relating to libraries and intellectual freedom. While getting bachelor's degrees in English and Journalism and a master's in Library and Information Science, she also studied philosophy, finding the philosophy of science and technology especially intriguing. She has contributed essays to *Doctor Who and Philosophy* and *The Big Bang Theory and Philosophy*. Like Holden, she wishes there were no phoniness and no ugliness in the world.

CHARLES TALIAFERRO, professor of philosophy at St. Olaf College, is the author or editor of fifteen books. Like Holden, Charles went to a prep school where he had a few dodgy teachers, he has a great sister, and at sixteen years old he took a train to New York City where he had some very embarrassing misadventures. Charles is not disclosing any further similarities.

JAMIE CARLIN WATSON is Assistant Professor of Philosophy and Chair of the Department of Religion and Philosophy at Young Harris

College in Young Harris, Georgia. He is co-author (with Robert Arp) of *Philosophy Demystified* (2011), *What's* Good *on TV: Understanding Ethics Through Television* (2011) and *Critical Thinking: An Introduction to Reasoning Well* (2011). He has also contributed to a number of popular culture and philosophy compilations, including *Johnny Cash and Philosophy, Transformers and Philosophy,* and *The Office and Philosophy.*

JAN WHITT is Professor of American Literature, Literary Journalism, and Media Studies at the University of Colorado at Boulder. She is the author of *Rain on a Strange Roof: A Southern Literary Memoir* (2012) and *Women in American Journalism* (2008). She teaches American literature, literary journalism, media studies, and women's studies. Known as a lunatic herself, she likes the guy in the Bible who lived in the tombs at least one hundred times more than she likes the Disciples.

Index

DOCTOR WHO

AND PHILOSOPHY
BIGGER ON THE INSIDE

EDITED BY COURTLAND LEWIS AND PAULA SMITHKA